The Early Posthumous Work

The Early Posthumous Work

ESSAYS BY

Steven Barthelme

RED HEN PRESS | *Los Angeles, CA*

The Early Posthumous Work
Copyright © 2009 by Steven Barthelme
All rights reserved

"Gamblers" from *Double Down: Reflections on Gambling and Loss* by Frederick
and Steven Barthelme. Copyright © 1999 by Frederick and Steven Barthelme.
Reprinted by permission of Houghton Mifflin Harcourt Publishing Company.
All rights reserved.

Book layout by Sydney Nichols
Cover image by Arian Camilleri (www.dripbook.com/ArianCamilleri)

Library of Congress Cataloging-in-Publication Data
Barthelme, Steve.
  The early posthumous work / Steven Barthelme. —1st ed.
     p. cm.
  Essays.
  ISBN 978-1-59709-388-0
  I. Title.
  PS3552.A7635E37 2009
  813'.54—dc22
                              2009031767

The Annenberg Foundation, the James Irvine Foundation, the Los
Angeles County Arts Commission, and the National Endowment
for the Arts partially support Red Hen Press.

First Edition

Published by Red Hen Press
Los Angeles, CA
www.redhen.org

Acknowledgements

The author wishes to thank the Mississippi Arts Commission for their generous support. Special thanks also go to Kaye Northcott, Ken Hammond, and Eric Copage. And to Mark Cull and Kate Gale, my gratitude and my admiration for the work they do and have done for years.

Grateful acknowledgement is made to the publications in which these pieces first appeared, sometimes under different titles or in different form: *Texas (Houston Chronicle)*, "An Ironic Dog's Prospects," "Snakes, Snobs and Sanctuary" (also in *State Lines*, Texas A&M University Press), "The Christmas Tree Fort War," "Off to Work We Go," "Fancy Girl," "The Back Porch," "Out There, Lucky and Loose," "Now We See Us Now We Don't," "Fan in Exile," "Second Best Friend"; *New York Times Magazine*, "Pop? In a Hat? C'mon," "Proust at Lunch"; *New York Times*, "Beautiful Deuces"; *Texas Observer*, "A Thirty-Five Year Old Book Review" (as "Chicago, Chicago"), "Random Telephone," "Kung Fu Defended," "The *Newsweek* Short Story," "Celestial Puzzler," "Don't Move: A Memoir"; *Apalachee Quarterly*, "Louisiana, Home of the Blues"; *Buffalo*, "Just Passing Through"; *Chronicle of Higher Education*, "Some T.A."; *Connecticut Review*, "Not As I Recall"; *Elle Decor*, "A House of Ideas"; *Los Angeles Times*, "Urban Farmer, Amiable Crop"; Nation Books *(These United States)*, "Mississippi: Idiosyncratic, Incomprehensible and Air-Conditioned"; *The New Yorker*, "Gamblers" (also in *Double Down*, Houghton Mifflin Co); *Oxford American*, "I Do, I Do"; *Washington Post*, "You Easterners Aren't Bad at All"; Writers Digest Books *(Rules of Thumb)*, "Enough Already."

For Joan,
who taught me much
when I most desperately needed to be taught,
and who foolishly admired
some of these things way back when

Contents

A Cubist Take on Teaching

Thousand-Word Wisecracks

I

Kid Stuff

An Ironic Dog's Prospects

All my early life I was told things were going to change, that who I was as a boy was not who I would be as a man, that nurture was more important than nature. This was nonsense of course. I learned so from a dog. In the Westside Houston neighborhood where I grew up, there were three boys around the same age, and we each had a dog. You could pretty well tell who we were by watching our dogs. Each dog bore not a physical but an uncanny spiritual resemblance to the boy who was his master. One dog was white, one was red, and one was black.

The white dog, whose name was Frisky, was not pure white—put a little black and brown around one ear, on his legs, and maybe some on his tail. Frisky was a medium-sized dog with the face of a fox and the temperament of an Englishman. He had a highly developed sense of propriety and prudence, and like any good Tory dog, was at all times ready to say so.

He had a strongly developed sense of property, too. This meant that Frisky would yap viciously as you walked up the driveway to his screen porch, and then abruptly shut up and lose interest when it became clear that you were not an intruder. It's possible he would have done the same thing if you were an intruder—Frisky was prudent to a fault.

His name suited him, because he was frisky, cheerful, with jingling tags and a stiff little body and the bounce in his step that marks some medium and small dogs' gait. Few things fazed him. He was an optimist. Frisky saw it more or less the way my friend seemed to see it—all was for the best in the best of all possible worlds.

In other words, like the family who loved him, Frisky was a Republican. My friend, son of the family and master to Frisky, seemed to move in some world invisible to me, a world which made sense. They had silver napkin rings over there, etched in Old English script with family initials. Oak boards lying around in the garage. We were not alike, really. My friend was even-tempered, friendly, contented. I had for him that awe that the unkempt feel for the well-groomed. How did he do it? Like Frisky, he had confidence. Like all good Republicans he later became a millionaire.

The red dog's name was Fang. Fang was a handsome devil, an Irish setter with long, silky rust-colored fur, long thin legs, tricky brown eyes, and graceful as a cat. He loved to run and to chase things, especially the big squirrels running overhead in the tops of the pine trees which shaded the neighborhood lawns. Fang was a prancer. He would head off at a dead run and then stop abruptly, both front legs thrown out to one side, almost like a horse, leap up again, and tear off in some other direction.

We lived not too far from a bayou, and when we went down there, while the other dogs were sniffing along the water's edge, Fang would splash right on in, then paddle around proudly in the muddy water. We worried about him, but he never had any trouble, and when he got back on the bank he was happy to shake the water out of his long darkened fur, spraying it all over us. As his name suggests, Fang was a free spirit, the neighborhood's canine libido. It ran in his family.

My childhood friend, like his dog, was never afraid of risks. One wet morning some years later when we were in high school, I was riding with him in a car, heading up a freeway ramp in the rain. I can still hear his voice saying, "Watch this!" as he gunned his little convertible, trying to cut in front of another car. We spun across in front of the other driver, off the entrance ramp, slid backward in the mud for twenty feet, and then spun around the rest of the way and fell eight inches or so over the curb onto the access road we had left a few seconds earlier. We looked at each other. Blinked. He later became a pilot.

My own dog had short, black fur with a white patch in a Bat-Signal shape on his chest, a docked tail two and a half inches long, and floppy ears. He looked like a small, rueful Labrador retriever. His name was George, a too cerebral name thought up by people too inclined to irony. But he was a cerebral, ironic dog. He was always trying to figure things out, often failing, full of doubt, bewildered. I felt the same way.

The two things George liked best were fighting and howling. He got along fine with Frisky and Fang, but any other dogs that wandered along the street were challenged if they set foot on George's yard. The small ones, oddly, George let off with a few snarls or sniffs, but the big shepherds and retrievers, and especially Weimaraners, for whom George had a particularly strong dislike, always required a fierce, flashy dogfight, teeth and claws, and rolling around on the grass. And often, a post-game trip to the veterinarian; George liked to fight, but he wasn't particularly good at it. Unfortunately there was a sort of fad for Weimaraners around this time, so until he got older, he made a lot of trips to the vet.

George's howling might be set off by some other dog in the distance, or the air-raid siren they used to test at noon on Fridays, or any other noise with a similar tone and rhythm. Sometimes we'd even start barking and howling ourselves, to encourage George. Then he'd settle back on his stub tail and throw his muzzle in the air and let out a long, deep, mournful howl, rising and falling slightly in pitch, complete it, and then start again. After a few good howls, he'd look around, as if shocked or embarrassed.

What George always did was worry. Even now his image comes back to me with troubled brown eyes below furrowed brows. When he first showed up as a stray in the neighborhood, he was already a head case, with a tendency to shy as if anticipating a blow. This was a time when jets overhead would sometimes rattle the windows with sonic booms, an event that always petrified him. Fear is as terrible a thing to see in an animal as it is in a person, and a special sort of fear comes from bewilderment, from not understanding, confusion, worrying, thinking too much. So a great deal of my childhood was spent telling George that yes, everything really was all right. It's all right. It's all right. It's all right, boy. It was good therapy for me, too, saying over and over this thing I didn't believe.

George was nervous his whole life, just like the white dog was frisky and the red dog was a democrat. Fifteen years of gentleness and reassurance never eased his psychological makeup, the irony in his genes, and the scars of the beatings and whatever else he had endured before he arrived in our neighborhood, running free with another black dog, a three-legged companion, who subsequently disappeared.

Little by little, George grew to trust us, within limits of his own determining. Little by little he became less likely to cringe at a loud noise or a sharp word. Little by little he got older and grayer. But he always worried. He never really changed. Which I guess is why now, almost thirty years thereafter, I'm not a pilot, or a millionaire.

Snakes, Snobs and Sanctuary

Now those other classes—upper class, lower class, writer class—make me uncomfortable. Once, when I was actually loose inside the River Oaks Country Club, for a friend's wedding, every time I looked up, cops were watching. Or so it seemed. On the other hand, my time in low-life circles where casual acquaintances tend to get killed or carted off to Leavenworth I happily kept to the minimum. Such silliness, part of the male writer's job description, makes the company of writers unspeakably dreary. Blah blah, nine millimeter automatic, blah blah, 115 miles per hour, blah blah, single malt whiskey. I prefer the middle class.

The problem is that the middle class has always made me uncomfortable too, even when I was ten. All those folks, edgy, trying to find things other people didn't like, so as to have "taste." All those folks, fretful, trying to talk hip, think quick, dress right. Worrying about each other's shoes. All those folks watching all those folks. It was hard to breathe. So, at ten, we hunted snakes.

This doesn't mean we stumbled onto the odd snake now and again. This means we chased those slinky devils all over Harris County, as well as Brazoria, Burleson, Waller, and other counties whose names I have forgotten.

I say "we" because snake collecting was a joint venture with the kid from across the street, a tall boy called J. E. B. Stuart (not his real name). Jeb was Episcopalian and I was Catholic, he was a fan of Robert E. Lee and that fluffy horse and I defended Grant (my mother was from Philadelphia) and booze, he went to public schools and I went to parochial, and as it was the middle class—we were fast friends.

Where Jeb and I couldn't get on foot or bicycle we had to be driven, by a handy parent or sometimes by an adult snake person. I remember standing out in Addicks beside a dry creek bed, sun streaming through the leaves of the trees, with some other kids and the khaki man who had brought them, looking at rusted soft drink cans, beer bottles and scraps of paper, the man saying, in a voice rich with disgust but also horribly dispirited, as if the vulgarity he witnessed had been targeted at him personally, "Civilization. Civilization." In feeling morally superior to litterers, he was, of course, far ahead of his time. We, backward, laughed at him behind his back.

We didn't catch anything that day, as I recall, but on other days we did. Once, near a small farm that Jeb's people owned near Caldwell, we found two beautiful six-foot Texas rat snakes, or "chickensnakes" as the locals called them, or *Elaphe obsoleta lindheimeri*, as Linnaeus would say. That I can remember their Latin name thirty years later illustrates how seriously we took our herpetology. A Texas rat snake is a big, thick-bodied, tan to gray individual marked with large brown blotches. We caught these, a yellowish one and a very dark dude, in an old feed shed, the one under a hay bale, the other in some burlap sacks. Jeb and I were ecstatic. I felt better that day than on the day, years later, that I sold my first book.

Another day we caught three speckled kingsnakes (*Lampropeltis getulus holbrooki*) in a field where Rogers Junior High School now stands. On many more days the catch was slim or none, and on others the work of snake ownership—feeding, cleaning out cages, manufacturing cages, keeping records, corresponding with other collectors in other states—kept us off the trail.

Most of the time we didn't wander so far afield. We were lucky to live off South Post Oak Road near a part of Buffalo Bayou which by now I'm sure is under several trillion tons of concrete and smoked glass. Caught in a gentle arc of the bayou was a large area of sand and willow trees and what I guess was limestone, and in among all of these were a half dozen shallow rain ponds the size of cattle tanks. There were even a couple of tiny spring-fed streams. To us this steamy, muddy, mosquito-filled swamp was the clear manifestation of God's bounty. The place was the Amazon of ribbon and garter snakes, world head-quarters for Blanchard's and yellow-bellied and diamondback water snakes, and it was ours.

Some of those summers we went to the ponds practically every day. The next street over from ours was one block long, re-cently paved, but unused. At the end of that, you ducked under a barbed wire fence, and followed a thin path through tall yel-low weeds under a few pine trees, the path running diagonally across the field to another string of barbed wire. Past that there was a steeply declining red clay "road" or at least a place where a bulldozer had once been. A thousand yards down this road were the ponds.

So every day, our sticks and old pillowcases in hand, we would head under the wire, across the field, under the wire, and down the clay road. When we got there, it was hours of painstaking study of each inch of the margin of a pond, or the shallow depths of a stream, slogging foot by foot along the banks, often stopping and staring, although staring doesn't really get it done. Stare, and you miss things—a certain curve, a bullet-shaped head looking out from weeds, someone red and yellow and brown hiding mo-tionless, in plain sight, under the rippling water.

It stays with you. Twenty years later I got a teaching job, at a rot-gut university in Louisiana. At a party, my host, one of my new colleagues, took me out back to show me his prize tomato vines. I reached out to the nearer bush, grabbed a green snake, and held it up. My new friend jumped. "How did you see that?" he said, back-pedalling. He never stopped talking about it. When I left Louisiana for a better job, a tiny professorship, my girlfriend and I had to return a beloved pet, a Graham's water snake, back to the slithering grounds where we had found him.

Last I heard, Jeb had made good in the meteorology business, securely in the middle class to this day. My professorship has made a great many people, notably my family, happy, by making me middle class again, after fifteen years of life without insurance. Middle-class adulthood is easy compared to middle-class childhood, which, I now realize, reptiles were a major factor in getting me through.

Snakes were outcasts, underdogs, losers. No one liked them, and while that didn't give us taste, it did give us an area of expertise all our own. And we found snakes out in the fields and barns and bayous, in so doing escaping not only the scrutiny of our parents but also the suffocating middle-class self-consciousness. There was no one among our acquaintances likely to come along and know better. And there was no one to judge our clothes or our slouches or our slang as we dug around under rotting logs or tramped through blonde fields or stood silently on either side of a shallow, cluttered, clear stream, looking into the water, hoping.

Christmas Tree Fort War

The last thing we did every Christmas season was to build our annual Christmas tree fort. After holiday dinners and gift-giving were over, and with school still a week or, with any luck, two weeks away, the inevitable boredom set in and we got outside. It was cold the week after New Year's, so we were usually wearing two or three shirts, and sweaters and heavy coats as we went around our southwest Houston area neighborhood and then into neighboring neighborhoods begging for their Christmas trees. At some houses, where the tree was still up and functional, we would secure a commitment for the tree once it was defrocked, agreeing to return in a day or two.

It seems odd now that after being showered—sometimes only sprinkled—with toys and books and rain gauges and trains and whatnot that we so quickly abandoned all that to get out into the mind- and finger-numbing cold weather and collect from the neighbors their discarded Christmas trees. But that's what we did.

Several neighborhood boys made up our group but the principals were three of us, my two closest friends, whom I will call Curley and Moe, and me. We dragged the trees back to Curley's front yard and then made our forts, engineering miracles of a sort, built on unsound principles often, but always creating a new, private space where none had existed before. Fortification was a big concept of my and my friends' childhood, I'm not sure why. It probably issued in part from the movies and TV shows we watched, things like *Davy Crockett* and *Daniel Boone* and Westerns about remote cavalry posts, but there was also probably something about the idea of keeping a wall between ourselves and other people, especially those most intrusive of other people—adults.

Sometimes the trees were piled into rectangular walls, knit at the corners, like Lincoln Logs. But usually we didn't have enough to do that, and the fort I remember best was the one we built and rebuilt one particular bitterly cold year, the year of the Christmas-tree fort war. The year we learned adult occupations like spying, duplicity, thievery, breaking and entering.

It started out innocently enough. We wandered around going from house to house, knocking on doors, sometimes not even knocking, just dragging off an obviously discarded tree lying out for city pickup. When we had enough, we set about constructing our fort, which that year was designed as a sort of tepee, the Christmas trees upright leaning against a big pine tree, angled a little so as to create a diagonal space circling the base of the pine. It wasn't a very tall space, but we weren't very tall people, and anyway, we were used to crawling, crouching, and so on. The architectural principle was that of the snail shell. On the outside of this we piled more and more trees, until our walls reached a satisfactory density, too thick to see through.

Our pleasure was all in the building of the fort, really, because once built, there wasn't a lot to do with it. You could hide things—like new Christmas presents—in it, but other than that, the fort threatened to become boring, that intolerable state which, to a child, lurks around every corner, and in the backseat of every car trip. Happily, that year, having finished our Christmas tree fort, we were attacked.

One morning the first week of January, Curley arrived at my door at some hour too horrible to contemplate, say 8:00 a.m., with the terrible news that our fort was gone. Gone, I said. What do you mean, gone? Come look for yourself, he said. Somebody stole it.

We knew who it was. Another group in the neighborhood had built their own pathetic, inept, tiny, ill-engineered, hopeless excuse for a Christmas tree fort in some kid's yard a block down and a block over. They didn't have enough trees and they had no know-how. It was a mess. Obviously, racked with envy, they had turned to crime. So we did too. First, we reconnoitered.

We looked all over the neighborhood, starting with the site of their shabby fort, now empty. We checked out the homes of each member of the rival group that we knew of. We followed the needle and tinsel tail, at least as far as it led us, until it somehow vanished, I assume into the back of someone's older brother's pickup truck. This took a couple of days.

It was Curley again (I think he had an informant) who found the missing trees, locked inside a big white storage shed behind a garage beside a big white house. Peering through a small window in the side of the building with our flashlight, late at night, we wanted our trees back. My friend wanted to go in right then but I persuaded him that maybe just after daylight might be safer. I never liked stealing things at night; it somehow made you more guilty.

So one January morning at about 5:00 a.m. we took a pry bar to the little window, which gave way with practically no resistance, and then jumped in and stole all our waste Christmas trees back. Nowadays such thievery might result in a fatality or two as the nervous homeowner unwinds with his .357 Magnum, but this was an earlier, and in some ways better time, when the general level of urban paranoia was lower and the readiness to kill each other over garden hoses and parking spaces was less immediate.

We dragged our trees back, at least down the block, and threw them into the back of Curley's older brother's pickup truck and drove them home. Just like San Francisco after the quake, or Rome after its sack, our fort rebuilt was even better than before, as we had acquired in the larceny not only our own old trees but a fair number of theirs as well. For a few days after, we even had the delicious luxury of standing watch to prevent them from repeating their crime, the pleasures of paranoia, an ailment which at least makes you the center of attention. But they never came.

Still, in this way, for this one year we managed to push back the scourge of boredom almost to the very morning we had to go back to school, there to endure the tedium which we had resigned ourselves to for the next twelve years or so. Boredom, of course, isn't a terrible problem to an adult, adulthood being at its heart the slow-motion collapse of all one's hopes and dreams, a certain age by which we have accepted ennui as our daily bread, but to a child, boredom is torture, hell itself, a feeling which requires a whole art to evade. I think sometimes this is why one writes. It's a way of never growing up.

Pop? In a Hat? C'mon.

In early August 1947, my father turned forty years old; I was zero. Actually I was about a month old, and being a slow child it had not yet occurred to me what being forty years younger than my father might mean. When I got to be ten, he would be fifty. There were four other children, three older brothers and an older sister, and so, at one month, I was probably busy listening to their advice, on the one hand, and defending myself on the other.

It was much later that I understood that my older siblings had had childhoods different from mine. It first dawned on me on a visit home after college, when I had dragged out the home screen and the old Bell & Howell movie projector—cast iron, steel, and glass and heavy as an artillery shell—and cued up some of the family films from the handsome, heavy wood box which had been stored in a closet.

My father was an early and accomplished amateur photographer, and the home movies he took date back to the thirties. To me it was perhaps more impressive that the movies ended in the early fifties, when I was about five, and he about forty-five. Sometime in those years he lost interest, or energy, or both; now, not far from forty-five myself, that doesn't seem surprising.

But it was not only the fact of these movies that struck me, years ago, when I watched them for the first time as an adult. It was their content.

There, on reel after reel of eight millimeter black and white, were my brothers and my sister, teasing dogs, reading books, playing baseball and football, opening Christmas presents, and splashing in the surf at the beach. They apparently went to the beach a lot. A number of these home movies had titles, elaborately arranged "plots," single-framing, and other tricky business. A surprising effort, in terms of the energy and attention, had clearly gone into their making. Especially the earlier ones. As the dates grew more recent, the films grew fewer, the filmmaking more perfunctory.

Late in this archive was some footage of the neighborhood on the far west side of Houston where I grew up. Now I finally understood what my parents meant when they said that, when they had moved out there six years before I was born, the place was a prairie. Great trees I knew only as adults appeared in the movies as scrawny little saplings. If they appeared at all.

The films, many having acquired a sepia tint, recorded my grandparents as middle-aged and overdressed, getting in and out of cars which to me were the stuff of legend—the Lincoln Zephyr, and several Studebakers, only the last of which, a green one, I could remember. They recorded my mother, young, almost girlish, trying to wave the camera aside—a classic shot in family films—and then giving in and laughing. And they recorded a young man, standing beside one of the cars, or swimming, or swinging one of his children around, or wearing a hat (a hat!), or sometimes racing to get into the picture, and smiling more than I ever saw him do. Who's that? I thought, but I knew who it was. I had just never seen him before.

I've known my father only as a middle-aged and an old man. He doesn't swim. He wears no hats. There hasn't been a lot of going to the beach, or fishing, or playing catch in the backyard. We played chess. Although he took a lot of still photographs, he had quit making movies. What I recall him making most was work. My father is the world's champion inventor of chores; once, we made a rug. Likely the reason I remember with fondness all the home repair and remodeling projects, the fetching of tools and even the homemade philosophy which always accompanied these jobs, is that this constituted my acquaintance. This and the dreaded "serious talk." He was always a great talker.

There was a lot of talk, and a lot of it was about age, and all of that reflected the folly of being young. I remember when my father told me my thirty-five-year-old brother was "going through a phase." (Later, I decided he was right.) Still I resented and resisted this sort of talk—it wasn't hard to see to whose advantage it played.

Being a child of older parents also contributed to the sense I always had, though not till recently quite understood, of having been born in a suit and tie. It was not so much, as I had always thought, a desire to be serious, but a desire to be older. By the time I was ten, not only were my parents fifty, but my oldest brother and sister were in their mid-twenties. Adulthood was the only game in town.

I lost this game, over and over, of course, and soon learned to spend much of my time with neighborhood kids wandering around in nearby swamps and fields and creeks.

My freedom to forage for a place and companions and even a way of being was a consequence also of my parents' age—they were probably not inclined to do such a thorough job of my upbringing as they had done with my brothers and sister. They had probably learned that there's such a thing as too much attention to the problem.

At forty and after, they had probably learned a great deal. What they had learned is what they told and taught me. On the rare occasions that I envision becoming a parent myself, this is what I think about: I'd rather not be the child of the man I was at twenty-five.

This, I thought, is what it means to be born when your father is forty and already has tended to several other children. The fine edge of his interest in the project—child-rearing—has grown a little dull. After all, the fifth time one does something is different from the first or second.

More to the point, he is a different person at forty than he was at twenty-four, or twenty-six, or thirty-two. There's no disputing that he is tired, less energetic, more set in his ways, less idealistic, less enthusiastic. But with luck he has also learned things, giving him different things to say. One talks a different talk after forty.

My brothers and sister did have a different sort of childhood. But, if my father and I played chess instead of baseball, if he took me to the hardware store instead of to the beach, and if when I knew him he made work instead of movies, still the man I have known was fifty, and fifty-five, and sixty-five. A wiser man than their father.

Not As I Recall

Jerry was my mother's sister's husband, and I knew him only distantly, for he and my aunt lived up north while I grew up in Texas, so I only saw him on two long vacations my mother and I spent at "the farm," a few hundred acres in southeast Pennsylvania where he raised corn and hay and a small herd of Black Angus cattle. I was eight and later ten or eleven on those vacations, so while I saw little of him in fact, I saw a great deal of him in imagination. In some sense, then, what follows is not true. But in some sense it is.

My father was a brilliant and demanding man whom I had always loved dearly; my uncle was like him in some ways but not in others. Jerry was a little older than my father, about fifty-five, tall, on the gangly side, with a penchant for browns and flannel shirts, and in his strong, tanned hands and his light eyes and his reserved, wry smile, I saw an ease as sublime as it was unfamiliar. Other men I knew were edgy, tightly wound. Jerry looked like a farmer, or at least what I knew farmers were supposed to look like, in all the folklore concerning farmers. He was wise, gentle, and kind.

Jerry died sixteen years ago, and I had lost contact with him for twenty years before that. My acquaintance with him was all a child's acquaintance, so what I have of him now is a few memories and images. His hands, for instance. Twelve or fifteen cats lived on the farm—house cats, strays, barn cats, and Jerry's cat, a big, scruffy old orange and white tom short an eye and half an ear. Evenings, the cat would settle in his lap as Jerry sat out on one of the porches in a rocking chair, and I can still see his hands' slow, automatic work, his hard fingers deep in the fur of the sleepy cat's bull neck.

His voice, too, was special, a deep voice with a smile in it. I knew irony, but the irony I knew, even when it was friendly, was unmistakably a weapon. This was a musing sort of irony which he was giving away to whomever he was talking to. He liked foolishness and play. He had grown up an orphan, in a home for boys, and so he probably knew a lot about nonsense and had a fine appreciation for it. Or maybe Jerry just figured that about half of everything everybody says is nonsense, an idea I understood much later.

His voice had an authority, too, when he chose to use it, to explain to a Texas city boy why we were turning the hay that morning, or how to handle his .22 rifle, or how to distinguish different breeds of cattle, or why I was not to bother my aunt. When he said something, I listened. But more often, he listened.

The .22 was one of a closetful of guns, but as far as I know Jerry seldom used them except when his nephews were up from Texas. He may have hunted in the winters, or when he was younger. In any case, guns were part of the exotic aura of the farm. At home we didn't have guns, though my friends' fathers and older brothers did. I stood beside the corn crib, shooting at a line of empty coffee cans. Jerry would stand behind me and to one side, coaching, and I thought he was the Rifleman or Buffalo Bill. I suspect now that he only saw what I wanted him to be and obliged.

Back home I spent much of my free time out of doors around the yet-to-be-developed bayous and fields of the raw Houston suburb where my family lived, but it was a suburb, nonetheless. The rolling fields and thick woods on my aunt and uncle's farm were better, with tractors and cows and barns and clear springs where the water just bubbled out of the ground. No doubt in some measure Jerry got blended in my imagination with the wonders of his property. He wasn't really even a farmer, except to me, and to himself.

I spent my weeks on the farm looking for snapping turtles and black racers, damming up creeks to make pools, and fooling around in the barns, looking up an empty silo for the slow white and gray owl that hung out in the top and would fly if you made enough noise, or spending hours playing on top of the hay bales stacked to near the tall ceilings. One never-used barn was full of airplane parts from some failed business deal, in an unconsummated state forever. There were some things I recognized, like propellers or the glass circles to cover the faces of gauges, but most of it was strange hardware which resisted identification.

I have no idea how he ended up with all that stuff, or what he eventually did with it. It was probably some get-rich scheme that crashed and burned. As a young man he had been trained as a carpenter and a patternmaker, but by the time I knew him Jerry made his living as a contractor, building houses in New Jersey and southeast Pennsylvania. He wasn't a farmer except as his heart was in the farm, the farming, and the cattle. The farm was sort of an idea he had.

Still, the farm work meant long days. When we were there, in summer, the hay was full grown and it was usually time to mow it. Then the wait, after it was cut, for the hay to dry enough so it could be baled and brought back to fill the barns for the winter. Each day after dinner, before sunset, I would go out to the fields with Jerry. There I watched him walk through the yellowing hay, stooping to pick up a handful here and there, checking the color and dampness underneath. A happy man. Watching him, I liked the easy, adult way he knew things, the knowingness.

Later I rode on the tractor pulling the hay rake, drawing the whole field into long concentric rows, in which the hay dried some more. Later still I worked beside Mike, Jerry's hired hand, on the flat wagons drawn in the noise and dust behind the baling machine, grabbing bales chugging out of it, using hooks, stacking bales in the pattern Jerry prescribed. We took the load back to a barn, and threw the bales on a conveyer for the ride up inside. The conveyer was John Deere green, with a moving belt down the center of a rickety triangular steel bed or channel maybe twenty-five feet long, reaching up into the loft of the barn.

I got to speak a new language—"silo" and "John Deere"— and to imagine myself a different way on Jerry's farm. Sometimes he stood behind me and let me sit in the driver's seat, driving the tractors. Sometimes I'd fill them up with gasoline from a large tank out by one of the barns. I drank from the springs, fed the cattle. Once when we were putting the hay bales up in the barn, before the conveyor was cut on, I walked up the long steel bed into the hayloft, an act of daring I had seen Mike do.

Jerry had no children of his own, which was suggested at the time (by my mother, I guess) as the explanation for his extraordinary gentleness toward my brothers and me. But I think that that ease was just his character, a mix of confidence and patience. It was (still is) a seductive style of meeting the world. My father was never an easy-going sort of man.

For me, the ruling image of Jerry is not so much an image as a feeling of his presence—always standing behind me, while I was driving the tractor, shooting the guns, arguing with the cows, occasionally offering me some tips, but letting me do it, whatever it was. He stood close enough to help but not so close as to imply that help was needed. Perfection was unlikely, maybe not even desirable. In that standing back, he gave me some of that sublime confidence he had, and I knew I could do it, too.

But that's not the end of this story.

Some years ago, the last time I tried to write about my uncle, I called my mother long-distance to ask her some questions about Jerry. My mother was eighty-one. It was a disturbing conversation.

She couldn't answer my questions. She told me—though her memory was failing—that this wasn't so, that that never happened. He was not an orphan. She didn't know anything about any barn full of airplane parts.

"Sure, Mom, don't you remember? There were three barns and the last one was a long low building, farthest from the house."

She said no. "Honey," she said, "you're confused." And other things, I had it all wrong. It wasn't the way I thought. I was stunned, defeated.

There in my kitchen I hung up the telephone in shock, holding onto this new, bewildering wound, a discovery, if it was a discovery, which shook me far beyond reason. Why be so troubled by the dispute of a handful of facts, things I'd never given much thought concerning someone long dead whom I hadn't seen in thirty years? I set aside the thing I was trying to write about my uncle, because I clearly didn't know what I was doing.

Time kept passing, a dozen years since that telephone call. What I think now is that Jerry is, and probably always was, an imagining, a man I made up. There are photographs—he was a wry, lanky, tan fellow, and the brown shirts are there—and past that, my brothers tend to recall him the same way. But Jerry is finally only an idea I had, an idea more dear than the facts. I'll likely never know for a fact if he really was wise, gentle, and kind. I don't know who he was; I only know who he is.

Off to Work We Go

My mother died a few years ago, at eighty-seven. As a young child, I had been very close to my mother and spent many hours accompanying her through her daily routine. Even though it wasn't glamorous and held no novelty, she seemed to like her work, days taken up with ordinary things like shopping and cooking and housekeeping. She ran errands. She worked in the garden. She cooked familiar things like casseroles or roast beef or soft white-bread chicken sandwiches, rich with margarine and salt, which tasted wonderful. Sometimes I wondered why she put so much effort and art into these dull tasks.

Memories of my father are vague, at least until later. Later, when I was an adolescent, my father said, "Get a job." He said this repeatedly. I'm sure he didn't realize how opaque this order always seemed to me, how mysterious it was, how I hadn't the first idea of how to go about it. As well as singing the praises of work, noting the many ways it was good for me, telling stories to illustrate key points, he also patiently tried to explain the nuts and bolts of how work might be acquired, but I was sort of hopeless.

The result, in several of those summers, was that I would spend some weeks walking through strip centers, hesitantly approaching the woman behind the cash register at, say, a drugstore or a dry cleaner's. "You don't need any help, do you?" I'd say. "I mean, I'm looking for a job."

One time I actually did get a job, one of the best I've ever had. This isn't saying much, given that my employment history prior to my current teaching job reads construction laborer, store clerk, laborer, dishwasher, taxi driver, handyman, laborer, advertising writer. There were others, but I forget. The summer job I did get was working for a florist, delivering flowers.

This job was probably arranged through connections, someone my parents knew. It's a cinch I didn't talk my way into it. That's what you were supposed to do. That was the point of one of my father's stories, about a young man who had once come to his office looking for work and just before getting booted out the door started pointing right and left to things there in the office that he could do. "I could straighten out those tracings," the plucky kid said. "I could file all that mail. Those cartons need labels." Etc. He was hired. I did get it, the story's moral, but then as now I could no more do this than I could speak Apache or part the Red Sea.

Before I could even start my new job, I had to get a commercial operator's driver's license, which was something of a problem because my regular license had been suspended for speeding tickets and one that said, "contest for speed." So I wrote Texas Governor John Connally and pled hardship, explaining that my prospective job required me to drive. This was how you asked for your license back, according to the authorities. Governor Connally most kindly and quickly unsuspended my license. This was before he became a Republican.

So I went to work in the back of the florist's shop. It was a chill and damp place, with weird tools and special paper and wire and Styrofoam and stands on which "sprays" were built, all colored green. The place smelled terrific, rich flower scents floating in wet, air-conditioned air. My boss was a stylish, good-looking woman in early middle age. When I wasn't delivering, I was set to work at minor tasks around the shop. A side door led out where the broken-down white Ford Econoline van was parked.

When driving is your work, the streets eventually form a pattern of shortcuts, ever congested places, synchronized stoplights, back ways and alleys, ideal spots for illegal turns, and so on. Before long I could find any address or get any order delivered ahead of time. Inside the van I sat high, right beside the engine, which was always overheating, so that my equipment included a couple of gallon jugs of water with which to replenish the cooling system. It was stunningly hot in there and loud as I jounced and rattled up and down the streets, happy as I could be.

After a while, I started driving the van harder and faster, adding style to simple efficiency, slipping through tight spaces, whipping around turns, parking as illegally as possible. The only motive was to make the work interesting, but it had the accidental side effect of a "job well done."

I went to apartments, houses, hospitals, and funeral homes. Once I delivered a corsage to a horse at a stables. Hospitals weren't too bad, and the recipient was usually happy to see me, bringing someone else's affection and concern and breaking up the boredom to boot. At the funeral homes, people I met had an odd, artificially perky demeanor. It was their discomfort with death. They stepped lively, as if to prove that they hadn't died, that they weren't the star of the show. After a while, I began to walk that way, too.

I got to know the town, at least the Westside where the florist was, and compared to the other work I had done up to that point, getting paid to drive was like getting paid to play. In fact, compared to most of the jobs I've had since, that's still true. But oddly as I got older I got to like work, not in any way that my father's stories had prepared me for. I still hated the tedium and the repetitiousness and the confinement in one spot—even now, when I teach, I pace.

Driving for money, alone and unsupervised, clued me in, because it was easier to think about it, to understand what would drive someone to work harder than they had to, to make an art out of a chore.

No one works hard for his employer's sake, no work is free of dullness and repetition, and nothing is duller than work you don't care about. But that equation can be reversed: Not caring makes work dull. All I had to do was turn the work into an art. It's a trick I learned from my mother.

Even in her eighties, in the last years before she died, however much she loved to complain about it, what she wanted to do was her work, especially the cooking. One of the last images I have of her is carrying a roast to the dining room table, arms trembling with the weight. She wouldn't let you take it from her. And when she herself could no longer cook, she nourished a keen resentment for the housekeeper who came to cook and clean, who my mother said didn't "know how" to bake a potato, among other failings. She was kidding, of course, making jokes; that was her other art.

II

Second Best Friend

Fancy Girl, Fancy Car

The girl's name was Mary Jo McBride. She was what's now called "preppy" looking, a big-boned, brown-haired girl, with beautiful eyes in a broad, soft, perfectly featured face and an elegant, polished ease of manner. She was only sixteen, but she walked, looked, turned her head with a grace that would have been the envy of a grown woman.

She was smart, and smart-mouthed, droll, ready with an ego-deflating put-down, some seemingly tossed-off remark which you didn't completely grasp until after she was on to the next thing. Talking was a contest, and nothing much disturbed her sublime confidence in her own abilities. She was probably a rich girl, or sort of a rich girl. To me, she was wonderful. And miracle of miracles, I had her in the car with me.

The car was my father's 1962 Corvette, a handsome white devil with a blister red interior open to the sky, the convertible top stowed behind the seats, even though the sky threatened rain and here and there we ran through patches of light drizzle as we wound around the streets of what was then far west Houston.

This was the car I never was allowed to drive, officially because I wasn't covered on the insurance, unofficially because my older brothers had raced and wrecked the three earlier Corvettes my father had owned until he had gotten fed up. But that day, in a mood, my father had handed me the keys and said, "Why don't you take the car for the afternoon?"

I had earlier carefully nudged this mood of his into being by spending half an hour or so lovingly washing the car in the front yard, using a scrub brush on the tires and SOS pads on the whitewalls, and for the rest just plenty of water and rag and muscle. This was in the way distant past, well before Armor All, so interior detailing was done with a vacuum cleaner and maybe a little soap and water. Whatever, by the time I was through the car looked very cherry. It gleamed.

I'll admit to not knowing what I was doing, on both fronts. I didn't know how to drive very well, being about sixteen myself and especially uncertain in this fancy car I might have been behind the wheel of only once or twice before.

Worse, I had no idea what I was doing with her or how it was supposed to work. All I knew was that I loved her, and that you got the fancy girl and put her in the fancy car, and good things were supposed to eventuate.

The car's interesting or exotic qualities were supposed to sort of rub off on you, in her experience of the thing, so that she fell for you, or at least thought you worthy to, as Walker Percy says in *The Moviegoer*, "hold her charms in your arms." I was like someone who thinks you make dinner by putting a lot of cans on the kitchen counter—some steps were completely missing from my understanding. I did know that you were supposed to drive them around in the fancy car, so that is what we did.

"Where do you want to go?" I probably said.

"I don't know," she probably replied, wind in her hair.

I was not wholly without guile or resources so I drove out toward the western edge of Houston, which at that time was a lot of empty blacktop roads cutting through fields of tall weeds and the low man-made rises of the dams and waterways. A place you could toss a fast little car around some, which I did, probably a lot more timidly than I recall it. Mary Jo was impervious. The car didn't seem to be doing its work. I suspect that she wasn't susceptible to cars, that a thorough-going knowledge of brandies or a sojourn of ambiguous character in some Central or South American country would have served me better.

"That was when I was in Belize," I could've said. "I really can't talk about it. Like another Courvoisier?" Except that there wasn't any Belize at that time, and I really didn't like brandy, and my understanding of women was not even to the point that I grasped that there was one girl who was seduced by cars and what they represented and another seduced by what she read about in *Elle*, and that most of them didn't care about either, they were seduced the same way I was, by being liked and admired with enough intricacy that they felt not only liked, but understood.

But I didn't understand any of that, all I had was this car, and it wasn't working worth a damn. At some point as we were swinging back toward town, the drizzle now coming down enough that I had had to stop and put the top up, I was trying to stay in the game with her, trying to put her down sharply enough to seem a worthy adversary and therefore a worthy match, I guess. Her indifference was huge; it was Montana. I was working as hard as I could, flirting as well as I could, trying to imitate the supremely confident people from late movies like Clark Gable and Errol Flynn. They were always making fun of the girls, and the girls loved it. The girls would get mad and huffy, but it drove them crazy.

Anyway, somewhere in here I made the mistake of trying to make fun of Mary Jo's prodigious vocabulary. Maybe she had used a word like "prodigious," I don't recall. She did then use the word "fatuous"—this I remember vividly—to describe whatever I had just said, and as I didn't know what that meant, I did the strategic thing and renewed my attack: "Ooh, gee, wow, gosh golly, there's another big word. Get that from the headmistress?"

Now this is a very reserved young woman there in the other red bucket seat, a smooth, easy girl. And she was gorgeous. Clearly sensing that I hadn't a clue what the word she had used meant, she allowed me to go on a bit, and then said, in a quietly direct voice: "It means . . . [pause] 'fat-headed.'" I looked over at her. She was perfect. I would never hold her charms in my arms.

It was a class thing. She was of the confident class, those people who always know exactly what they are doing. Whether she got that way at Saks Fifth Avenue or at prep school or when Mom and Dad took her to Europe or when touched by the Holy Spirit, or whether she was simply pretending confidence, didn't much matter. Pretending, feigning it—faking it—I later learned, was the usual method; Margaret Thatcher, Bruce Willis, Captain Blood, that's how they all started out. The trick is to forget that you're pretending. That's the part I never managed. I could never get out of the Huh? class.

What happened? I wrecked the car. No big slam bang smash-up, just a sliding right turn on the glistening pavement, trying to get off Memorial Drive, a slide which ended against some woman's Buick. The Buick was barely marked, but the Corvette was fiberglass and got a little torn up. I stood there in the rain, waiting for the cops, waiting for my father, wondering, again, why I wasn't one of those lucky people who have all things under control. I still wonder that, most of the time. I didn't get a ticket; blame fell on the wet streets. Somebody took Mary Jo home.

Second Best Friend

Let's face it, love is not only blind, it's stupid. A man is always falling in love with someone who's too old or too young, already married, waiting for the light to change, or walking away across the airport terminal. One falls in love with shirts, screwdrivers, dogs, chairs, peanut butter and bacon sandwiches. And it has no fashion sense, love, nor any sense of timing. When all my contemporaries were embracing either Marx or money market mutual funds, some embracing both, I fell in love with a car.

I was twenty-nine before I owned an automobile, and the one I bought then, because it was eleven years old, cost me only four hundred dollars (I had to borrow half of it). It was the first thing of appreciable value I had ever owned, a green 1966 TR4-A, what used to be called a "sports car." The car was small, dirty, and loud, and a rectangle the size of a shoebox had been cut out of the clouded rear window of the convertible top so that one could see. "Roadster," the title said.

The day I bought it, I had handed over a check and waited in the seller's driveway while he telephoned my bank, then we signed papers, shook hands, and I was ready to leave. The guy started the car for me, leaving the hood up, then disconnected the battery with the engine still running, brought a different battery out of his garage and swapped out the one he had started the car with, closed the hood. Smiled. I thought, Too late now. And I really wanted this car.

So I had to buy a battery the next day, and the day after that, new tires. The tires were new only in the sense of being new acquaintances to this particular car. I bought them behind service stations and off the used racks at tire dealers for five dollars, five dollars, two dollars, seven-fifty. One guy crouched down beside one of the front tires, ran his hand over the brown cord showing where tread had once been, and said, "Yep, you're riding on air, there."

A week later, one side of the front suspension broke away from the frame, fortunately for me, not at speed. I found a guy in the phone book to weld it back. After that everything else on the car broke, too, but I loved it anyway.

That was a long time ago, but like an ex-lover, I could tell you in all the intervening years, even long after we had parted, where to find that car, the street address I mean. For fifteen years it was in Columbus, Ohio. Now it's back in Texas, in Fort Worth. I live in Mississippi. But I bought the car in Austin.

I had been thinking about buying a car for fifteen years, by that time. In high school I used to read the classified ads, looking for cheap XKE Jaguars and such, enjoying the thrill you get when for a split second the mind confuses wanting with having. I still do this, on occasion, and still get pleasurably confused.

I had good reason for wandering in the want-ads as a teenager, what with my mother's car, which was a highly visible old Oldsmobile, which even she was a little embarrassed at, an antique which had been my grandmother's. It was two-tone, fuchsia over mauve. I didn't have any money then (it's a chronic condition), so my shopping was idle. My mother allowed me to use her car while suggesting I get a job and buy myself my own. But money just didn't seem to accumulate for me the way it did for other people. I made peace with the double-purple Olds.

This happened in Texas, where like much of the country away from the East Coast, you pretty much couldn't exist without a car. Couldn't and didn't. Among young people, the car was an identity—"she drives that SuperSport," they would say. "He's the GTO." To give an address or directions to a house, we didn't talk about Tudor or French provincial and we didn't tell people what color the shutters were. We just specified what was parked outside—"there's an old Dodge on the street and a blue Mustang in the carport." Later we grew up. Sort of.

I went to college a year in Boston, carless, and that was of course no problem. Then I transferred back to the University of Texas in Austin and walked a great deal. After a year or two, a close friend of mine turned up with a used Triumph, which he was amazingly willing to lend me. Thus emboldened, I got a new girlfriend. Another year or two and my girlfriend got a brand new Volkswagen, a gift from her father for graduating. Those years seemed much longer at the time than they do now.

We drove the VW to California to have a new life, took it to see my friend with the Triumph, who had moved to Sunnyvale. We took a cat, and bought American flags for the side and back windows, as camouflage. Our new life lasted about three months, and then we split up. She went to Denver. I was back in Houston, staying at my parents' house, no girlfriend, no job, and worst of all, no car.

So after two months of that, I called her and flew up to get her, and we drove the VW back to Austin to live together for about seven years. We worked clerical and menial jobs, collected green stamps, were young. For a while, I drove a taxicab, a Checker. Because we were living on the extreme cheap, in those seven years I learned almost everything there was to know about that Volkswagen. I became not exactly a good shade-tree mechanic so much as a devoted one.

When we split up, she kept the Volkswagen. I was twenty-nine and emboldened by a new girlfriend, I bought the first car I ever owned, an eleven-year-old roadster, which I found one day while I was wandering in the classifieds. It was designated "Triumph $400." No model, no color, no year, and nothing about the battery or the tires. So I borrowed the other two hundred dollars and went out and bought it. I had loved the VW, but this was bliss. When my brother got me a job in Paris, I told him I couldn't go.

Instead I spent the next five years working on the Triumph. It was a very demanding car. Fix my timing chain, my shock absorbers need oil, overhaul my generator, water pump, master cylinders, starter, carburetors, clutch. This weather stripping's looking a little shabby, too. I'd like a new convertible top. Other cars have carpet, why don't I have any carpet? It was full-time intimacy.

I bought Triumph books and a torque wrench. I began saying things like "torque wrench," intoxicated now with a legitimate reason to use the jargon—title, roadster, clutch, locknut, big-end bearings.

Throwing a wrench around any of the thousand or so bolts on these obviously important items, I found, could drive the car-oholic mad with pleasure. Six or eight hours later, when you had irretrievably destroyed whatever it was you were trying to fix, your feelings were less pure. Heaven, I thought, was a place where there's nothing to fix.

There were other surprising pleasures to car owning, the largest of which was the powerful sense of independence which attached thereto. This showed up in everything from taking the top down to leaving your junk in the back seat as well as the lightly ecstatic feeling that you could leave and never come back. You don't ever go; it's just a feeling.

Ownership was a strange concept and looking it up in the dictionary didn't help, but I figured if everyone else insisted on pretending that they owned things, I might as well pretend, too. The psychological discomfort was nonetheless acute for a beginner. Try understanding the term "asset" when you've never had one—it was like coming down with parrot fever. Incomprehensible. Some things helped. The wrench work, of course, but I also discovered that a lot of washing or polishing of the possession, for example, made it feel more possessed. There were a dozen varieties of caresses.

Sometimes my ex-girlfriend would call me at 2:00 a.m., stranded in some place like the Albertson's parking lot when the

Volkswagen wouldn't start, and I would fix that one. I remember Albertson's specifically because I chipped my front teeth there holding a flashlight with them in twenty-degree January weather. Some time later my ex-girlfriend sold me the Volkswagen because I wanted it, because she needed the money, and because she had gotten another car. For a while there I had both cars in the driveway. My house was the one with the green TR-4 and the tan VW, and my new girlfriend's old blue Oldsmobile. By that time I knew a lot about the Triumph, and some about the Olds, too. It was one reason I needed the VW—to go get parts for the other cars when neither of them worked.

And then there was my girlfriend's little sister's car, a different model Triumph, a "GT-6," with much more engine than I had known about when I helped her pick it out. I spent some time working on that one, too. She drove it in a swashbuckling style ("What was that, a red light?") and I was sure she was going to hurt herself, and her fiancé, who I was getting to like, would never forgive me. Not to mention my mother-in-law. It was then a great relief when finally little sister graduated, got a job, bought a Honda. She agreed to sell the GT-6. One morning the fiancé called me in a panic to say they had a guy coming to look at the car and it wouldn't start, wouldn't even turn over. So I hurried over to their house and we pulled the starter out and rebuilt it in twenty minutes. Little sister married the fiancé. He and I became friends.

All this time, of course, I'm getting older. My girlfriend is waiting tables at a Mexican restaurant, and I'm working, in a desultory, very part-time sort of way, for my ex-sister-in-law's advertising agency. And I'm sort of over-age to be spending five or six years working on a car. My kin's untiring attempts to get me a job, as in a "real" job, have come more or less to naught. It's time to go away to graduate school. I borrow more money.

We sold all three of the cars, and bought a newer used Oldsmobile, a big yellow brute which would carry almost everything we needed. We paid nine hundred for this one, plus four more for a transmission. Borrowed money. My new brother-in-law, a saint, but more important, a saint with a chubby cash flow, bought the Triumph from me. We went down to the corner to get the title transfer notarized at a savings bank, and he politely looked away when my eyes started to tear up a little. I was embarrassed. After all, it was just a car.

That was years ago now. After I got out of graduate school and got a job at least nominally real, I borrowed some more money and bought a new car, a low little Honda Prelude, a clear if distant echo of the car I had loved, and spent five years paying that off. Later, three more Hondas. Nowadays two white ones out front, the older of which also has enough of that echo that I can't bring myself to trade it in.

My brother-in-law still has my old Triumph although he did move it to Ohio, and then to Fort Worth, so I don't see it much anymore. I hear about it though, now and then, long distance, and I remember what it felt like to be in love. And sometimes I think about it, about replacing the timing chain, or tuning the engine, or repainting the bracket which held the brake and clutch master cylinders, how loud it was, the way it smelled and shook, how I ran it up to a hundred miles per hour once on the Houston highway and later my mechanic friend said, "You really are crazy." That bracket was silver.

The Back Porch

I am not lost. The store, happily, has one aisle or wall which glitters with blister packs of nails, screws, electrical junk, duct tape, and tools: linesman's pliers and coping saws, screwdriver sets, wire strippers, squares, levels, wrenches. A supermarket's food or a drugstore's gaudy vitamins are too complex. I know, as I wander up and down the other aisles, that some of it kills you and some of it cures you, but I can never remember which is which. Neither, apparently, can the writers of most of the health articles I read.

The hardware is different. It doesn't matter that I don't buy it (buy cheap tools and you'll have to buy good ones later, my father told me) or that I already own most of these items anyway—it's a place to visit. When no excuse can be found to go to Sears or the hardware store or the car parts joint, the hardware aisle of a suburban drugstore will do.

Excuses are necessary because while I like my job, it doesn't provide spare cash for things like belt sanders, and because the only tools my work requires are a tweed coat and a red pen. Pleasant in their way, but they don't really satisfy. The best excuse I ever had was a car.

Living in Austin some years ago I bought a broken-down old British sports car, and then spent five years repairing it, from the ground up, as they say. In the beginning, I knew little about cars. But I was willing to learn and, only vaguely employed, had a lot of time to spend around repair shops, parts joints, and junkyards.

I replaced the rear axle. Rebuilt brake cylinders. Redid the interior. Stood in the weeds off Highway 71 amidst hundreds of wrecked cars, some piled one on top of the other, pulling important pieces of hardware from less fortunate old Triumphs. The great moment of my auto repair career came one afternoon at the shop of a mechanic friend when he looked at me and said, "You ruin your hands yet?" It was like being admitted to the fraternity. It was a fraternity.

I also bought. Ordinary things like box wrenches and locking pliers and fancier stuff like a torque wrench and a strange little device called a "Uni-Syn," which measures carburetor balance— a breathalyzer for carburetors. The pleasures of these things as well as of ratchets, locknuts, gap gauges, and what the British car books call a "distance piece"—a spacer—kept me going.

I inherited this affection in a way, as my grandfather was a lumberman, ran a lathe, and he and my father both built things they needed or wanted as a matter of course. My father's work was intimidating; I long ago gave up trying to do as fine a job making things as he did. Even so I have his abiding affection for tools, sit typing at a table I built ten years ago with my own saws, sanders, squares and screwdrivers. I should say, the third table I built ten years ago, as the results of my first two tries at table-making were too unstable or simply too ugly to bear, and ended up consigned to scrap.

But that's all in the game. Over time, having shared with these tools the healing of brake calipers and timing chains and carburetors, not to mention tables that wobble and door hinges that whine, one develops an attachment. A fierce attachment.

Once I loaned a friend some tools, saying, "Take good care of that; that screwdriver's been with me a long time." She did, and she returned it, but the phrase "been with me" stuck in my mind. It seems an odd way to talk about a screwdriver, let alone a two-dollar example with a bashed-up yellow handle, scarred shank, and less-than-perfectly-smooth tip. Here was the sick affection most people reserve for dogs and cats, lavished on a screwdriver.

Perhaps the remark would have made more sense if I had been talking about a hundred-dollar miter saw or power sander, or the power drill I got with green stamps thirty years ago when green stamps still existed. Or if the handle had been mother of pearl. Or if the screwdriver had belonged to my father, or to my grandfather. My grandfather has been dead for sixty years; his place in my memory is secured not by images of long afternoons of yarn spinning on the veranda but by my father's love for him, by photographs, and by his tools.

When my father's father died in Galveston in 1956, his tools came to our house. Heavy hand planes with blades sharp enough to shave with. Rakes and hoes and shovels, their handles dry and gray. A wicked hand scythe. Hammers. Pliers. A rasp. A pair of hand saws, one large and one small, their blades grown dark with age and, I suspect, oil. He took good care of his tools.

I was nine at the time, and I loved (and still love) the tools and their names. My grandfather's tools took their places easily among those my father already owned. Most went to the back porch, hung on the wall above shelves of coffee cans filled with nails and screws and all manner of small threaded and hooked and hollow pieces of steel only a few of which I ever learned the use or purpose of.

The back porch was a magical place, although it was much later that I understood quite why. Tools were not only powerful, they were also simple and direct in a way one's relations with the world and especially with other people, and most especially with women, were not. An Allen head wrench fit an Allen head screw. Special jobs required special pliers: needlenose. A great deal simpler than the girl who couldn't go out because her grandmother had died; after her fourth grandmother, I understood, and called some other girl.

One evening years later when I was lying underneath a car on a cool concrete garage floor, my hand on a five-eighths box wrench hooked around a five-eighths bolt, the reason I loved the grease and the cut knuckles and the grit which falls in your eye came to me. I thought: It's so damn clear. It was just a richer version of the feeling I had at nine on my father's back porch.

I have since seen these things—the tools on the walls, the shelves, the coffee cans (non-drinkers use jars, or tin cans, or whatever)—in the homes and garages and "workshops" of dope dealers and oil executives, mechanics and poets. I have come to recognize this as ordinary, even mundane. But to me, at nine, it was a powerful symbol of what one was supposed to do and be.

And more than symbols, the tools are a sort of refuge. With their quiet loyalty and clear and precise function, tools are comprehensible. They make sense. One's job, one's love life, one's emotions, even one's breakfast, often don't.

This explains why I took up auto repair at twenty-nine and spent the next five years fixing a car ("One car?" someone asked; I nodded), how a beat-up yellow screwdriver came to be less a possession than an old and trusted friend, and how it's possible for someone to lose half an hour or an hour at any fair-sized drugstore, and not be lost.

Out There, Lucky and Loose

When I was about seven, my father used to take the family to the beach at Galveston, a drive of about eighty miles from our home in West Houston. As we rolled along old Texas Highway 6, sometimes he would sing out the names of the small towns we passed, towns whose names seemed all to begin with the letter "A." This litany—Arcola, Alvin, Algoa—was one of the many things which made the trip an adventure. Coming back, tired, late at night in the dark backseat surrounded by the low sounds of the car, watching lights like pinpricks all around, I felt fiercely content.

Oddly, my most vivid memories of Texas are often memories of highway, and even now, when twice a year I come back, it's only when I get on US 10 and then on Texas 71 between Houston and Austin that an old feeling comes over me: yeah, I like it here.

Ten or so years after those childhood beach trips to Galveston with my family, fresh from a year at college in Boston, one afternoon I left my parents' house and headed for Austin, hitchhiking. I had never hitchhiked before going to Massachusetts, had only rarely seen hitchhikers in Texas, but it was commonplace in the East and my new college friends' principal means of travel. The highways up there seemed tame compared to ours, with the towns close together and few long, empty stretches of bare road.

I was a very green eighteen-year-old boy, but a girl I knew was in Austin. I left without saying anything to anyone and walked a few suburban blocks to the highway. I didn't know the way, wasn't sure which highway to take, started out at five o'clock in the afternoon. I was the only pedestrian out there, and more than a little anxious.

What amounts to a less-than-three-hour drive took me about eight hours. My first ride was with an old trucker, an easy-going, talkative guy who sort of adopted me on the spot. I had never been inside a semi before, so he got to tell me all about what he loved best. He dropped me off on the side of the road in a desolate spot somewhere before Columbus, and almost as soon as I got thumb up in the air, two cars pulled off just past where I was standing. Damn, I thought, I'm pretty good at this. I ran and got in the first car.

It developed that the six men in the two convertibles—a Cadillac and a white Thunderbird—were all traveling together. Did I want to go to Las Vegas with them? Their eagerness was unsettling, didn't seem quite right, but maybe there was nothing to it. When I didn't want to go to Las Vegas, they said at least ride to El Paso. Nah, sorry, I can't, I said, and when the seven of us were walking into a restaurant where we'd stopped a half hour later, I faded to the end of the procession and then turned around at the door and walked off down the highway.

Another trucker, a young guy who didn't talk, picked me up and carried me to about Bastrop, where I sat at a brand new highway intersection for three hours, ignored by the half dozen cars that passed during that time. It was an eerie atmosphere. In the streetlights, the new concrete and curbs were a white island with the odd, abandoned feel of brand new streets at night. Beyond the cones of light, the darkness was total. Sitting there felt like being in a terrarium.

After twelve midnight a car finally stopped, a beat-up Oldsmobile, loud, with the paint pretty much gone. It looked real good to me after several hours sitting around watching grasshoppers and moths catch the light when they rose briefly out of the weeds by the highway. I stood up and approached a little cautiously until a woman's big voice came from the passenger's seat, "Well, c'mon, honey, if you're coming."

I hustled over and got in the back seat of the car. The black woman who was talking said something I didn't catch to her husband and then, "Watch you don't tear you clothes on that barrel." Only then did I turn and see beside me in the dark back seat an old, rusty forty-gallon drum. There's no way I can convey the stunning sweetness which I heard in her voice, but twenty-five years later I remember the sound of it, her beautiful warning.

That was all. They gave me a ride the rest of the way, let me off on Martin Luther King, which then was called 19th Street, and I waited in a Hojo's for five or six hours until I could call and wake my girlfriend. I don't know if it is from that trip or a hundred later ones that I recall the way in the low hills the lights of Austin become visible and disappear, become visible again and disappear again as you drive in at night from Houston.

Since that time I have spent a lot of time on highways, driving across country, moving from state to state, coming back to Texas from a lot of different places. I got to know Highway 1 in California for a while, and there's a chunk of the Pennsylvania Turnpike I drove every week one summer. But (shocking to admit) the roads I like best lie between family and friends in Houston and family and friends in Austin, US 10 and Texas 71. Sometimes twenty-seven miles of Texas 95.

It's a route that doesn't have much character, really, and what character it does have I don't much care about. When a bypass was built around Columbus I rejoiced, and then when they added a bypass around La Grange that didn't bother me much, either, except that I miss the roast beef at the Bon Ton. What I associate with roads is not quaint settlements or breathtaking scenery—although I like the fields and scrub oak and mesquite and the cows that always look melancholy as much as I like breathtaking California or western Virginia countryside, just in a different way.

It's the highway mostly, being out there and loose that I care about. I like being in the car, rolling, and the memory of other rides with women I've loved, rides with friends, rides in ancient cars hoping the wheels stayed on and some when they didn't, even a trip I took once with a panting cat in an un-air-conditioned Cutlass when I had to stop and buy a bag of ice, wrap it in a towel and put that under him so the cat would stop acting like he was dying.

It's tiny things. I like snake farms, curio shops, even historical markers. I remember someone I had a ride with once in a crowded car saying, "Welcome back," when I woke from an unscheduled nap. I remember a girl who made me stop so she could pick wildflowers, bluebonnets of course, and some red ones I had never noticed before. I remember another night riding with another friend and blowing a tire and going into a roadside club called the Blue Flame to see if we could scare up a jack and a lug wrench. A highway north from Chattanooga where the fog was so heavy you tried desperately to hold onto some guy's taillights because you couldn't see eighteen inches past the front of your hood, a route I later found out was famous for that and for twenty-seven-car pile-ups. And one highway that ended—just ended—in Nevada, and you turned around and went back the way you had come.

I don't know why I remember this stuff. But there's something special about being out there. On the highway, you aren't where you were yesterday and you aren't where you're going to be tomorrow, which means in a way that you aren't who you are, you're somebody else. That's what I mean by loose. And if you're lucky, you hear that woman's beautiful voice.

Just Passing Through

I never felt much passion about furniture, except maybe about the futon, a sleepable, foldable piece of Japanese wizardry which I grew to hate. After months of sleeping on this cleverly disguised and attractively named rock, my wife and I finally bought a real mattress. Not a bed, mind you; a mattress. As for other big furniture, we've had to give it up. We like to move.

It was seven moves cross-country in ten years. So our luxurious furnishings can all be folded up, torn down, or stuffed into an oversize cardboard box: director's chairs, industrial-style steel shelving units, collapsible tables, and for carpet, room-sized remnants which can be rolled, folded, and slipped into a carton. The rest comes from the lumberyard. The dining table is birch-veneer plywood on a one-by-three frame. Desks, a platform bed, shelves—anything but chairs—can readily be fashioned out of pine lumber and plywood. Chairs, you buy, but make sure they're box-able. No Barcaloungers.

Once you have the boxes shipped and the car packed, you set out. This, of course, is the best part not only of the moving experience but of your whole life, the three or four days out on the highway with the cat lying around up on top of the blanket or bedspread covering the stuff piled in the back seat. He's up there chowing down on the few plants you managed to fit in—a starter set for your new place in Boston or Palo Alto or wherever. This is where the joy sets in, a few hours away from wherever you were last night. This is why for years they wrote novels the plot summary of which was "young man drives around."

We used to do this in a fifteen-year-old Oldsmobile which is not a method I recommend. Older cars are often big—especially if you leave the back seat with in-laws—but moving cross-country in one makes for a lot of anxiety about things like inspection stickers and wheel bearings. It makes for a lot of thinking, What's that clunking noise? It makes for colorful days spent cooling your heels (and the cat's heels) in dreary places like Roanoke, while they put a new master cylinder or engine in your car. It's for young people. No, your car should be no more than ten years old, preferably less. That way, you enjoy the scenery.

The country, passing by outside your car windows, is empty, beautiful. It's beautiful in one way in the West and a much different way in the East, but compared to what you are used to looking at—that is, mostly, architecture by F. W. Woolworth— the countryside's fields, bridges, rivers, mountainsides, trees, and creeks are breathtaking. I have been a city person all my life, in Houston, Boston, Austin, Santa Barbara, and Baltimore, and half a dozen other places. Still, every time I get out on the highway, I think, My God. Look at this. It's not only beautiful. It's not only, Look at this, but also, Look at all this room. For a second, the concept of a million people crowded on city lots, in apartments, in supermarket lines, seems ridiculous. Such thoughts last exactly one second, until I remember that life without supermarkets is not worth living.

The problem is, I suspect, that this experience of the countryside is only available to city people, and only when they're moving. The country person, suffering what Walker Percy called "the everyday" and the psychologists call "habituation," thinks of all this land as his own Woolworth's. He can't see it because he's used to it. A city person who isn't in the process of moving views the countryside as an annoyance, something suffered between where he has come from and where he's going, so he doesn't see it either.

But a person who's moving can see it, because for a few days, he or she is free. Roanoke is only dreary if you're stuck there, not if you're just passing through. In fact, the just-passing-through feeling is at the heart of the pleasures of moving. Just-passing-through is the exact opposite of "habituation," and so the reason why the mover not only can see the countryside but can see it as beautiful. And it's not only the "natural" parts of the scenery that benefit.

For years I used to hear educated, sophisticated folk complain about motels as a blight on our culture, prefab eyesores, palaces of plastic, and so on. I wondered why they thought motels were so awful, because I sort of liked them. Eventually I discovered a dark secret: a great many people like them. I am not talking about motels that are sleazy and authentic or rustic and quaint, but big shiny brand name places with glowing parking lots and ninety-channel cable TV and acupuncture showers.

The best ones aren't quaint at all, but as plastic as paradise. They're new, clean, characterless. You get some junk food and a Coke from the vending machines, some ice, tell the cat to hush, crank the air-conditioning up to flurries, kick back on the bedspread, read the local newspaper, or flip through your ninety channels. There is not a single thing here for you to worry about. Nothing for you to do. You are anonymous. Tomorrow you'll be gone.

Like other blissful feelings, this one is only temporary. And like a motel, the experience of moving is itself essentially transitory. Eventually, you have to get there, wherever there is.

Still, even after you've reached the new place, unpacked the car and the cardboard cartons, screwed the furniture back together, got your new birch plywood dining table up and bought a new mattress, benefits from moving linger. You're a stranger. It's not only the pleasures of discovering new places and people and supermarkets.

People tend to treat you surprisingly well, when you're new in a place. They all (we all) feel a little trapped where they live, and that feeling results in a special affinity for someone who has gotten loose, even if only temporarily. To them, you prove that their dreams of escape are not only daydreams. They look at you and see . . . Australia.

I recall stopping at a little store somewhere on a two-lane highway in Pennsylvania once, buying some cold Cokes and chocolate bars, and the weary woman behind the counter saying, "You're not from here, are you, honey?"—and then her stunning smile when I told her "Texas." Any place, New York or Idaho or Kazakhstan, would have done the same thing for her. Texas made it better, but it was "not from here" that made her smile.

III

C'mon, I'm Serious

House of Ideas

We were both back in Texas in the summer of 1993 visiting our parents, and one day on our way downtown my brother and I detoured slightly out of the way to see the neighborhood where we had grown up. It's a suburban neighborhood in what thirty years ago was far west Houston, just across South Post Oak Lane from where George H. W. Bush's new home was going up. We took a minute to look for George's house, too, but couldn't decide between the two houses being built on that short street. Further down, we turned onto Wynden Drive, the half-mile loop that was our old street.

The yards no longer looked familiar. The trees were too tall or too short, or their lower limbs were all gone, or they were surrounded by unfamiliar bushes or only the bushes that had surrounded them were still there and the trees themselves were gone. Trees stood where they hadn't been or they weren't where they had been. A lot of them had disappeared.

The varieties were the same—pines, mostly, and some willows, and Chinese tallow trees and small oaks. But the big double willow tree in front of our old house had been cut down and grown back smaller. A tall Lombardy poplar stretched twenty or thirty feet high out by the street. It was supposed to be in the backyard, just behind the house out the window of the bedroom where I had slept for most of my childhood. Right before my parents had sold the house I had taken some off-shoots from the backyard poplar and tried to transplant them at a rent house in Austin, but they didn't survive.

The house was hard to see. There was a new beige brick wall, taller than the old red one. The old line of crape myrtle down the right margin of the yard had grown to ten feet or more, and across in front of the house new plantings had changed the aspect of the place and obscured the house itself. We stared out of the car as we passed, turned around, stopped out front and stared, drove up in the driveway and stared. "Seen enough?" my brother said, and I nodded, but I hadn't seen anything.

Five years had passed since I was down that street and fifteen years since my father sold the house and twenty-five since I lived there. But it was my only home for eighteen years as a child and as an adolescent, so I don't guess I'll ever be able to see the house, except in imagination and memory.

The house my father had designed was an anomaly in a neighborhood of ranch style houses and a few vaguely Tudor brick two-story places. It was a large flat-roofed rectangle with one small square room standing up on top, somewhere around the golden mean. In the family it was described as "a cigar box with a cracker box on top."

More than geometry set it apart. The exterior surface was copper, a thick, penny-colored foil pressed tightly over lap and gap wood. If you stood back from the house it was a massive brown-gold thing looming over you up to the edge of the flat roof past which you saw only the sky. Closer, you saw the vertical channels of the wood underneath, and the mottled copper's small variations in color. The metal was thick enough to puff and ripple, giving the surface a delicate texture. Father had extra copper in fat rolls on our back porch. The copper had been supposed to turn green when treated with some chemical wash, but luckily, my family said, like many of father's ideas it didn't work.

My father studied under the great French architect Paul Phillipe Cret in the twenties at the University of Pennsylvania. Father tells a story about showing the famous Frenchman one of his first student designs. Cret looked it over and asked where the idea had come from; Father said, "I got it out of my head, Mr. Cret." Cret paused, staring at the tracing, and said, "It is good that it is out." This was one of my father's favorite stories; it also explained his own pedagogical style.

Subsequent work met with greater approval and a few years after he graduated in 1929, Father moved home to Texas to practice architecture. He became an early modernist, equally taken with Corbusier and Mies and Frank Lloyd Wright. So in 1941 when he borrowed some money from his father, and designed his own house to be set on the prairie outskirts of Houston, Texas, he also borrowed liberally both from Europe and from Wright.

The front of the house, with big windows from one end to the other, was protected by a six foot high brick wall with a wide opening off-center right and then an open garage. Between the house and the wall were a slightly raised front porch, a courtyard, and gardens. As a child, I helped my mother with the gardens, planting petunias, ferns, elephant ears, Dutch iris.

One old family photograph shows two or three of the children working these front gardens, and I'm bringing the wheelbarrow, at about three years old. There were always two or three of us at it; work was always done in concert. As the last of five children, I always felt that I had arrived late, that whatever it was I was the last to get in on it, even work.

At the back of the house, the two bedrooms off to the right each had a band of windows across the center of the back wall. Tall floor-to-ceiling windows formed the back wall of the rest of the house, looking out on a large brick terrace (which my older brothers and my sister had built, brick by brick, including a round brick barbecue pit at one corner) under a flat redwood roof. Gardens ran on either side of the terrace and along under the bedroom windows. Beyond that, the backyard.

It was handsome in its prairie Bauhaus way and had the supreme good fortune to have been built far enough out from the city that the land was cheap and the lots were large—"three quarters of an acre," I can still hear my mother saying—which left us with huge lawns front and back, full of the tallow and willow trees, the Lombardy poplars, and along one margin, a forty- or fifty-foot-long stand of bamboo that my father—ever the architect—had planted.

There was lots of yard work, too—raking and clipping and edging and so on. The neighborhood was full of pine trees, but we had none, a blessing I never appreciated until years later when I lived in pine-shaded houses in Louisiana and Mississippi, and spent half the year raking the needles.

I was actually disappointed when my father, after several lemons in a row, gave up on power lawnmowers completely and hired people to mow the yard sometime just before I was to take over this chore from the next-to-last brother. It felt like being disenfranchised. It was supposed to be a rite of passage. We still owned what everyone called a "push-push" lawnmower and there was lots of tall talk about the years my elder brothers had spent using this backbreaking device. The family lore was richly developed by the time I came on line, down to and including lawn-mowing lore.

Inside as well, the house was anomalous. I gave it no thought at the time, but the place was a sort of hothouse of modern furniture. It was not the same furniture as at my friends' houses. When my brother carved his initials in the arm of a chair, it was the flat bent birch plywood of an Alvar Aalto armchair. There were small and large Aalto tables as well, and two pairs of swooping Saarinen arm chairs, and the big rosewood and black leather Eames chair and stool—all the comfortable stuff out of the modern and Scandinavian catalogue. In the townhouse apartment where my parents later lived, they still used all the furniture they managed to prevent their children from stealing. In my living room today I have the worn old Aalto chair with my brother's initials.

Other furniture Father designed and built himself, or had built to order, or else had us build under his supervision. Cabinets, bookcases and a big square redwood coffee table and a screen wall we built which was covered in moleskin hand dyed in delicate browns and grays and golds. One major piece was what we called the lounge. In its first incarnation it was a flat, fat, backless couch covered in a nubby black and white fabric. Later it became a long low couch covered in an off-red fabric and incorporating white Formica end tables as part of the design. I always admired it, but my father spent years thereafter drawing sketches, redesigning this lounge. The new one would be better, he said. We never built it again, but I kept one of the sketches, which is itself beautiful.

In the house, there was an open spiral stair to the second floor room that was reserved as the bedroom for the oldest child at home. The upstairs room was finished in redwood, with two big wood-framed sliding glass doors opening onto a deck where well before I was born they had played shuffleboard. The outside of the upstairs bedroom was covered in copper like the rest of the house.

Downstairs were three bedrooms, a playroom, kitchen, and a darkroom, and in the center of everything a big open living area. The ceilings were nine foot, and in the main living room, which was about forty by twenty-five feet, one interior wall was brick and the others were redwood. The back wall was windows, and the natural light and the high ceilings gave you a sense of being loose. "Enclosure," my father always complained. "It's not natural." Even those windows that didn't go from floor to ceiling were four feet high.

I say all this, as if it were always so. In fact, these things are like snapshots of memory, because in this house, things were forever changing, being perfected, and it was us who were changing them. Before the back wall became fixed windows, it had been massive nine-foot-tall wood-frame sliding glass doors. Before the long counters in my mother's kitchen were yellow Formica they were a gray zinc. Central heat and air came late, and we put in the last of the ducts ourselves.

I remember one sweltering day with my father, trying to fit a big galvanized piece which was to split the ductwork into two channels feeding the two long ducts in the back bedrooms. It was late in the afternoon, the thing was very heavy, the house was hot, and the work had to be done on a ladder and overhead. "Let's quit," my father said. I looked at him. He had never quit before I was ready to before. "It's hard tonight," he said. "It'll be easy tomorrow." Of course he was right.

My father the architect was always having a better idea, and he had five children, an ever-ready workforce. Maybe the reason that this house has taken on mythic dimension in my imagination is not only that I grew up there, but that in some small way, like my parents and my brothers and sister, I built it. Over and over. When we talk it's always, "Remember the terrace?" "Remember the barbecue pit?" "Remember the rug?"

As the last of the five children, I probably missed several incarnations of the flooring of my father's house. I vaguely remember black linoleum tile, and then a sort of red-brown linoleum tile on top of that. I better recall the tatami mats we put down sometime in the fifties and the black fabric tape which we ironed down to cover the joints between them and the way the black fabric didn't hold and the mats tore and had to be repaired or replaced. They were nice, but they were trouble. More and more and more tacks went in to hold them. Finally, after some years of this, we pulled them up and put down new white tile in their stead. But what I remember most vividly is the rug.

Father couldn't just go out and buy a rug like other people. He had to make one, which meant we had to make one. It was about twelve by fourteen, and assembled from three carpets, cut in long strips and attached to one another in a repeating pattern. First was a three foot wide strip of a soft, white cut pile, next a ten-inch wide strip of a beige carpet with a low, thatched-looking texture, and then a one-inch wide strip of black-brown loop pile stuff, and every three feet, the pattern began again. This, too, was handsome, set at one end of the big open living area between the front wall and the windowed back wall, lying over the ghosts of those ornery tatami mats.

I remember one of the people who came to look at the house when my parents were selling it called one day to say would we mind if they brought "their" architect by to check some things out. He was a pleasant, stooped man in a brown suit with a tape measure. As I watched my father, he gave no hint of being wounded as they traipsed around the house he had designed almost forty years before, the house he—and we—had been building ever since. I was wounded. "Architect" meant something else to me.

What all the rest of this means—the rectangle with a square on top, the copper walls, tall windows, terraces, bamboo, the slinky furniture, the work, the rug, and the rest of it, and the phenomenon that each thing came encapsulated in a comment or remark, some special lexicon or family lore or joke—is that the place I grew up in was not so much a building as a structure of ideas.

They were ideas about how things should be—simple, elegant, with no thirst for attention; and ideas about how people should be—lucid, imaginative, and ready to laugh when they outsmarted themselves, which was most of the time; and most centrally, the idea that everything could always be better than it was. Anything was possible. All you needed was the willingness to care.

After my father and mother sold the house, it went through several owners and was eventually torn down. Something was built in its place. Condominiums, most likely. My parents are gone now, too. All the furniture was distributed, given or thrown away or sold.

Like any late arrival to a philosophy or a code, as a child I was powerfully taken with the ideas inherent in the way they lived, the house we lived in. I still am. They were lovely ideas, I think now.

Now We See Us, Now We Don't

When I was growing up in Houston, there wasn't any *Dallas*. No *Miami Vice*, and no *Designing Women*. Watching television in those days, you could get the impression that the three places into which the country was divided included its two cities—New York and Los Angeles—and the Wild West. The TV seemed not to know that there were, or had ever been, cities down south. With a selection of other TV fare ranging from Perry Mason to Perry Como, Ed Sullivan to Edd "Kookie" Byrnes, it was not surprising that my best friend and I might look to the many Westerns then being broadcast for a friendly or familiar attitude or accent.

Even though the closest I ever got to horses was watching them out the car window on highway trips, I could still identify with Westerns, in which the word "Texas" was spoken again and again, usually with a drawl. Sometimes they even got the drawl right. Larry McMurtry writes somewhere of noticing that cowboys were the number one fans of cowboy movies, a phenomenon which I suspect is more general than that. I mean that it's not limited to one's occupation. I'm sure they're up there in Fargo (and Minnesota) watching *Fargo*, over and over.

As a child, though, I had an allegiance not only to Westerns but to any show set east of Los Angeles and south of the Mason-

Dixon line. Drama, comedy, news, it didn't matter, as long as Texas or Houston or at least the South figured prominently in it. In fact, Hurricane Carla was about the biggest TV show one of those years, special because it meant the country was watching us, rather than us watching them. Ordinarily we had to search much harder to find ourselves on TV.

One of our favorite shows was set in New Orleans. *Yancy Derringer* was a half-hour series starring an actor named Jock Mahoney, whose interpretation of the lead role owed more than a little to Clark Gable's Rhett Butler. The series appeared in the late fifties, and that year my friend and I assumed the roles of the insouciant gambler and his silent sidekick, as they plied their trade in the Big Easy before it was called the Big Easy. My friend was older, so he usually got to be Yancy Derringer, there in his living room, and I played the stony-faced Pawnee companion, Pahoo, which I privately thought the better role.

Yancy Derringer was an aristocrat and a dandy, and didn't do much but play cards and romance women in gigantic dresses, but every week he managed to get into some kind of jam, usually arising from his exaggerated Southern sense of chivalry. Then he'd have to rely on his namesake, the derringer pistol which he kept in his hat. If that didn't work, it was time for Pahoo, his faithful Native American companion, to show up and get Yancy out of trouble.

Pahoo, played by X. Brands, tended to settle matters with a sawed-off shotgun, which was a big part of his considerable charm. He had once saved Yancy's life, and, according to the show, Pawnee etiquette required him to keep on saving it for as long as the series stayed on the air. Not long, as it turned out; *Yancy Derringer* ran for only thirty-four episodes (according to Wikipedia), which makes these two characters' place in my memory seem all the more remarkable—maybe that should say pathological.

In the years that followed, new shows caught my attention. Some Westerns, but there were others as well. Several were set in New Orleans, such as *Bourbon Street Beat*, which lasted a year, and much later one of the best-written TV shows I've ever seen, a brilliant sitcom called *Frank's Place*, which was a critical success but a ratings failure. Once I even found a show set in Houston itself, a series pilot called *Hernandez, Houston P. D.*, in which they talked of Telephone Road and such, but the pilot wasn't picked up and the series never made it onto the regular schedule. That was shortly after Ryan O'Neal and Jacqueline Bisset made a film called *The Thief Who Came to Dinner*, not only set in Houston but filmed partially at an apartment my brother had lived in, briefly, the year before. The apartment's role amounted to a door shown opening and closing, if I remember right. *Sic transit gloria.*

In the sixties I went off to college in Boston and for a while my interests turned away from TV to movies. When I should've been studying or sleeping, I was up watching the late show and the late late show and the one after that. Of course, I favored great old films about the West and the South, in most of which cities didn't figure much, either. I watched everything from *Giant*, *Band of Angels*, and *Hurry Sundown* to more arcane movies like *Claudelle English* and *Written on the Wind*. That Texas or the South looked odd, and looked odd in pretty much the same way in all of these movies didn't bother me—at least it was home. When the place you come from is interpreted by moviemakers who don't really know it, it's going to come out looking strange.

Even in much more contemporary films like *Urban Cowboy*, *Terms of Endearment*, or *No Country for Old Men*, the Texas on the screen tends to look less like the place you know than like that place you've seen over and over again in old movies and TV shows. Although, come to think of it, they probably can't make a movie which accurately draws Hell's Kitchen or Hollywood either. I'm not sure that matters, anyway.

Still, I suspect most Southerners develop a heavily ironic attitude toward the images reflected back to them by movies and television. At Boston College one day, one of my new friends asked, "Do you have paved roads in Texas?" I looked at him real careful for a moment to make sure he was serious, and then in the thickest drawl I could conjure, said, "Yeah, but the goddamn Indians keep tearin' 'em up!" He nodded very thoughtfully.

In a minor key, this inclination has lasted into adulthood. Even now when I watch the evening news, I'm tuned for stories about Texas or Mississippi, the places I've lived the longest. When I watched *Homicide* or *The Wire*, I kept an eye out for the Baltimore streets, shopping malls, liquor stores, or landmarks I knew in the two years I lived there. The power of television is in part the power of confirmation. If your place doesn't show up on TV, you don't quite exist. We knew that when we were nine.

As a child I never cared if the picture wasn't quite accurate. But I wanted them to certify my part of the world, that it was here, that it counted just as the Naked City or Sunset Strip did. In Texas you learn early on that no one ever quite gets the story straight, especially our Northern brethren. You sort of expect folks to get it wrong. But you want your spot on the schedule nonetheless.

Fan in Exile

You might not know the plight of loyal sports fans before the advent of XM radio and streaming video, when to be from a city, Houston, for instance, and displaced, and dedicated to the perennial runner-up sports teams of that city meant an endless quest for game broadcasts or even a little footage. I have credentials. I used to watch the Oilers with Blanda. I remember Moses Malone and Calvin Murphy, Curley Culp and Billy Paultz. Dan Pastorini. As far back as the fifties, I listened to Loell Pass's radio broadcasts of the Houston Buffaloes. Luis Aparicio at short. I've never seen a Rockets game or an Astros game or an Oilers game in person, and haven't lived in Houston in thirty years. So what? I'm still a fan, and this is what it was like.

There must have been thousands of us out here, lost souls, wandering the TV channels, praying for another miracle, a superstation game, Astros against the Cubs or Rockets against the Hawks, or waiting for the Saints to fall so hopelessly behind that the network switches games, or hanging on for the half-time report hoping for some tape of Warren Moon or Hakeem Olajuwon or Jeff Bagwell. Meantime, we read *USA Today*, and wait.

My life as a lost fan began in 1965 when I left Houston for college in Massachusetts. For months I listened to my new friends blathering about U Conn and St. Johns and Providence in Yankee accents. They asked questions: Don't they play basketball in Texas? Hockey? Long about March, I discovered myself to be a great fan of the University of Texas at El Paso. Somewhere around March, 1966, the UTEP basketball team reached first in the national polls. I cut the rankings out of the *Boston Globe* and taped them up at eye level on the double doors between wings of my dormitory. Adopting an El Paso school was cheating, of course, but for all my friends knew, El Paso was a Houston suburb, just out Westheimer Road. Maybe I told them it was just out Westheimer. UTEP won the national championship. I transferred home. In 1970, I moved away a second time, and since then, it's been worse.

There was that eighties National League Championship series that we watched in the office, in a thicket of Mets fans. A night driving around town, looking for a hill where the car radio would catch a Rockets playoff. The afternoon we listened to twenty-five dollars' worth of an Oilers-Browns game on the long distance telephone. The videotapes, overnight mail. The pain, the pain.

One fall Saturday we spent fifty-five dollars on a TV antenna about the size of a canoe, then on Sunday morning rounded up thirty feet of pipe to get above the pine trees. After bolting the antenna on top, I climbed up and crawled around the roof for a couple of hours, raising the antenna, twisting the pipe, shouting down, trying to pull Jackson, Mississippi, or Alexandria, Louisiana, both stations, the *TV Guide* said, carrying the Oiler game. Back down on the ground, on the kitchen floor—our antenna wire was too short, and wouldn't reach the living room—eventually we did get a snowy glimpse of a field, and two teams. One was the Oilers—the announcers said so. A breeze would come, or maybe just some wobble in the Van Allen Belt, and the screen would go to sandpaper, the audio to fuzz. We saw two or three plays. I gave the antenna away, decided to go to high technology.

The first miniature satellite dish was pretty high tech, the early type of mini-dish which one aimed by the seat of one's pants. It was only thirty inches across, but we had a magazine article which said they worked. Ours didn't work. After spending hours out on the driveway aiming at the sky where the satellite was supposed to be, we had no picture. We drove around, looking for other people's massive dishes, to see where they had them pointed, went home and aimed some more. Maybe the receiver or the LNB was defective. Whatever, we never got more than a flash of light cutting through the snow on the screen. (Several seasons later we would get one of the newer mini-dishes and solve all our problems; the season after that, the Oilers moved to Tennessee.)

The next year we didn't go to Wiggins, not even once. Wiggins, Mississippi, thirty-five miles from where I live, is an eerie, dark place, a town of a thousand or so where they haven't yet discovered the streetlight. I know this because I got off the highway and lost there one night, looking for a Houston Chronicle box that someone had told me was out front of a hamburger place. The reason I wanted the Chronicle was, of course, the sports section. We never found it.

But we used to go to Wiggins on many a Sunday afternoon, to a motel which had Channel 6 in New Orleans and Oiler games not carried locally. Our local station shows Miami games. We had tried calls, threats, disguising our voices—and got more Miami games. So we took to driving down to Wiggins. The game that I remember was Oilers and Cincinnati. With a minute to go, our boys went ahead on a fluke ninety-yard fumble return. In the final minute, the Bengals waltzed down and scored. The motel room was bright yellow, as I recall, and it had, over the sink, an "industrial strength" air freshener, in a little bottle, like nitroglycerine.

I wish I was making this up, but no. I wish I could turn tail and take up another team. Some you could never like—the Jazz, for instance, or the Mets or the Spurs or Cowboys, or any team from Philadelphia. But what about the loveable Bears or the lonesome Orioles?

It's not like there haven't been opportunities to switch. I lived in Boston in 1966, a year the Celtics won the NBA, and in Baltimore in 1983, when the Orioles won the World Series. No, we've been loyal to a fault.

This morbid allegiance to sports teams of a city where I haven't lived in thirty years is weird, but by no means uncommon. At the office, here in Mississippi, there are Celtics fans and Mets fans and Cubs fans and Bills fans, as lost as we are. Somehow this link with a city is precious, a twentieth century badge like the brand of beer you drink or car you drive or an accent that miraculously grows thicker the farther away you get from your childhood home. So, we search the alien airwaves for stray Oilers or Rockets or Astros games, thinking Super Bowl, NBA Champs, World Series. So far, in vain.

What I propose is taking all that talent and making one team. Maybe if Houston only tried to compete in one sport, instead of two or three, your lost fans out here would not have to sneak past acquaintances from New York or Denver or Detroit, or, God help us, Buffalo. Play Craig Biggio at point guard, Mike Scott at shooting guard, Hakeem at fullback, Drexler on the mound. Linebackers, Bagwell and Billy Cannon. Munchak. And Otis Thorpe, Charles Barkley, Kenny Smith, Ray Childress. Luis Aparicio. Yao. Earl Campbell. Elvin Hayes. The Big E. The Snake. The Big Cat. White Shoes. Worth a try.

You Easterners Aren't Bad at All

They said, Go East. See the glittering cities, the towering intellects, the tony sophisticates. So we did. It was easy. Most of the traffic was going the other way.

We left friends and furniture behind and stuffed the rest of what we owned into the heaviest Oldsmobile ever to leave Texas. Hit a rat in Louisiana and beer cans in Alabama and left them all flatter than Kleenex. Cut a corner off Tennessee, got well lost in Virginia, found Maryland. We ate NoDoz and chocolate bars and noticed how empty and beautiful the country is. The cat, a good cat, slept the whole time in a cardboard box. On the fourth day we discovered Baltimore.

We are still discovering Baltimore.

How stylish, how chic, not to put up street signs. Or put them up crooked so a poor boy can't tell which street is which. Or to bring nine streets together in the Ballmer version of an "intersection." Let's not forget streets which go from four lanes to one to six in the space of three blocks. A French philosopher did the city plan, right?

We fled to Washington, an island of Eastern sanity, we thought. Erroneously, as it turned out. While laid out by a Frenchman, the place is now obviously controlled by lawyers. How else explain the hundreds of instructions, prohibitions, bills of particular and technological advice to the lovelorn displayed at every corner on D. C. street signs? "Face Out Parking/Red Cars Only." And, "Tall Women 3:30 – 4:00 p.m. Use Reverse Gear."

Now back in Baltimore, I'm getting used to it, and I must admit, the locals really know how to give directions. "Take Maryland Avenue to Fayette Street, hang a right, and pull into the used car lot. Your suspension is shot. Buy another car." In Ballmer, we get about twelve miles to the gallon and several hundred yards per shock absorber. Where exactly did you all learn to pave?

At first I was surprised by the free and easy way the descendants of Poe and Mencken use their horns. At the slightest provocation, Baltimore's Buick's honk and Mazda's tweet. It's nice actually, but at first I didn't understand. Then I remembered Houston, where if you honk at someone you better be sure and have the .38 out of the glove compartment. Just in case.

Random notes. The print in the local newspaper is a trifle dark, it's almost art deco. While we tone down the paper, could we also tone up the city wardrobe? Balto-style—brown meets gray. We could siphon off for the wardrobe some of the stunning imagination used in creating the local liquor laws. We buy by the case now. Who knows? Beer may be illegal in December.

The people of Baltimore are agreeable, but not carelessly friendly. Smiling's not real big here. It's all that sophistication and refinement. Life's grim business all right. At the grocery store, a big thinker in a housedress dashes into the eighteen inches I foolishly leave between my basket and the checkout counter, and I think, Yes, every second counts in Ballmer.

To one coming from a primitive culture, the sophisticated East can be bewildering. What, for instance, is the correct length of time to wait while a salesclerk, secretary, or sandwich-slinger yaks with his or her boyfriend, girlfriend, regular customer or dope dealer? Back home, all our dope dealers always stop and say, "Can I help you?" I know, I know, it's old-fashioned. An equally old-fashioned sense of fair play prompts me to record those things about Baltimore a stranger notices and likes. Maybe even loves. It's a seductive town, everything else notwithstanding.

There are roofs and sometimes whole buildings the likes of which I've never seen. It's great to be in a part of the country where the tacky has had a hundred or two hundred years to age into the charming. We walk the streets, gazing up.

The pizza is superb, even richer than the architecture. There are other things. Every other street corner has a bench, every bench the melodious legend: "William Donald Schaefer and the Citizens of Baltimore." Sounds like a country song. And one morning, downtown, I saw a guy walking down the sidewalk with two five- or six-foot snakes, one in each hand. Pythons, by the look of them. Just some guy out walking his pythons. A woman behind a cash register advises us not to apply for her department store's credit card: "They want to know too much," she says. Another woman, another store, when someone jumps ahead in line: "Get back there. People gotta respect other people's rights." And the Bromo-Seltzer clock, fifteen stories high, which will probably always be my private icon of Baltimore.

Thinking about that clock, this afternoon, kicking my way down a broken sidewalk hidden under scarlet and yellow leaves, it occurred to me: it's not at all bad here, not like they told me, it's hardly different at all. Just don't forget the mayor's name, don't criticize their baseball team and, for God's sake, don't ever say anything about their city.

I mean, of course, our city.

Proust at Lunch

If you stay in the writing business long enough, even in the marginal way I have, eventually almost all the people you know are writers. In general, they're good company. True as well, probably, of pet shop owners or postmen or parachutists, but years ago the idea of a life among artists seduced me. I imagined living and working in the midst of sophisticated, good-looking men and women who savored delicate phrases and sipped delicate wine, bet on horses, quoted Macaulay, tossed off occasional brilliant remarks concerning nearby architecture, and in general lived a fuller and finer life than other people. In among these foolish, B-movie ideas was one good one—that sophistication meant behaving with a certain style, or grace.

Early on I discovered a second idea of what sophistication meant, which had to do with knowing, ranking, and buying. A sophisticated person could, say, distinguish Honduran mahogany from African mahogany, and explain why one was better than the other. The knowing was always about quality, and the proof that you knew was what you had bought. So you owned Afghan rugs, French wines, Italian suits, and German cars. That is, you planned to buy those things after you became successful. Meantime, you just went to Pier 1 like everybody else. Quality always seemed to come with an accent.

One day several years ago, an incident suggested to me how completely the second definition has superseded the first—what you know matters, how you behave does not. It was at a day of meetings, and I was at a restaurant for lunch with three other writers. It was a minor incident, hardly worth recording, but I can't seem to forget it, and fueled perhaps by guilt that in this tiny commerce I didn't show myself well, in fact didn't show at all, I turn it over in mind sometimes, and want to tell about it.

It was a bad day all around. After a late flight, I had managed only two hours sleep the night before, and at breakfast, at 7:00 a.m., I was talking to the toast. But by lunch I was feeling, if not better, at least more stable. My companions—a woman and two men—seemed congenial.

The woman was dark-haired, soft-spoken, and acute. One of the men was a tall, bearded guy with quick wit and eyes. The other was a clever, genial man with several books to his credit, a man—his friends kept telling me throughout the day—who was a free spirit, a rebel, an innovator, whose work was not bound by convention or limited by bankrupt forms or published in New York. Evidence for all these heroic traits was offered in the form of anecdotes which his friends had clearly retrieved and saved from occasions the rebel himself had dropped them. I should have read his work, but I hadn't, so I took their word for it. In any case, there the four of us sat. I seem to remember some heroism having been displayed in securing us a table, but maybe that didn't happen.

The waiter came. He was a surpassingly clean-cut kid in a starched white shirt, slightly bovine, tall, with a pleasant smile and a burr haircut, and he was about the most polite individual on the planet. It was all Yes Ma'am and No Sir, and I'm sorry, sir, and No, no trouble, not at all, I'll check with the kitchen. As he stood beside the table talking—or rather, listening—no strain was evident in all this deference, no servility in his young face. He was a true believer, and what he was believing in at the moment was his job, and past that, that adults were the older and wiser ones, so if a mistake was made, it was surely his.

After some chitchat with this remarkable kid, we ordered drinks. I was tired, and afraid to drink much, as I had a show to put on shortly after lunch, so I probably asked for a beer. I don't recall what the woman and the bearded man had, but the rebel's drink is the only one which is germane. With some fanfare, and speaking with maybe heroic care, he ordered a "single malt whiskey," stopping the boy after; to make sure he had heard and understood the significance of this specification. He did not, as he might have, name Glenlivet or Glenfiddich or whatever, just "single malt whiskey."

Long ago I had read, like any other apprentice writer, those Hemingway books in which drink and knowing about drink are suggested as the mark of truly cultured and sophisticated people. I was as fond of the jargon of bars and drinking—barback, lush, call liquor, well liquor, bourbon up, water back—as the next phony. I had a dim idea of what a "single malt whiskey" was, but only a dim one: single malt whiskey costs two or three times as much as other kinds. I didn't drink it.

In the privacy of my own life I drank what is known derisively as "supermarket beer" or "lawn mower's beer." The quality was low, but the price was quite lovely. I also had heard of a marketing study in which drinkers, blindfolded and served four brands of beer, including the one they usually drank, couldn't tell them apart. When I now think of what I should have done at lunch that day, that study is what I think of. A what-I-should've-said thing. I wish I had ordered four glasses of four different whiskies, handed the rebel a blindfold, and challenged him to pick out the "single malt" variety.

The waiter came back, delivering our drinks, and set one on a napkin in front of the hero. He looked up sharply, that is, without smelling or tasting the drink, and said—sharply—"What is this?" It was so automatic that I guessed that the whole thing had been a set-up, that he was hoping against hope to be served a blended whiskey. But perhaps he was just being extra careful.

The kid smiled, stood beside the table looking down, apprehensive. "That's Johnny Walker Black, sir." Even I knew that was wrong. The kid shifted his weight.

The hero sighed, looked at the boy as if talking to a cow. "I asked for a single malt whiskey," the hero said, and then he sighed again. "You don't know what a single malt whiskey is?" He leaned back, just a little, as if to devote his full attention to this matter. "Here," he said, with elaborately feigned patience, "take this back." Then he looked around the table at the rest of us. For congratulations, I suppose.

I'm afraid that's all of it that I remember well enough to quote, but double it and you get a rough idea of the contempt and humiliation that the artist hero thought this ignorance, this breach of taste and culture, merited. He eventually got his fancy whiskey; the waiter went on serving with as good grace as before, even elegantly, under the mathematical definition of elegant as having no unnecessary elements.

Once I read in a book a description of Marcel Proust at lunch, who, having tipped his own waiter, then worried that the other waiters might be hurt, and tipped all of them as well. Once I found in a dictionary a definition of "sophistication" as "the absence of grossness." It made me happy; that's what I wanted "sophistication" to be. I still have the dictionary and sometimes I look the word up again, so as not to forget what it means.

Mississippi:
Idiosyncratic, Incomprehensible,
and Air-Conditioned

The other day we stopped by Sam's Club to pick up one of their rotisserie chickens, and two young butchers were standing back behind the counters shooting the breeze when we walked up. The nearer of the two guys, who looked to be Indian or Pakistani, asked if he could help us, and I said, "Well, we were wondering which of these—" I waved at the plastic boxes on stainless steel shelves under the heat lamps—"which is the most recent to arrive here." "They've all been set out within the last half hour," the guy said. My wife and I looked at each other, examined the chickens, which all looked pretty savory, discussed a couple in detail, hesitated. The butcher stepped up and selected the last package on the upper row of plastic boxes, and lifted it slightly. "Carl," he said, "would be an excellent choice." We took Carl. This is Mississippi, 2003.

Another day last week, as we left the Home Depot parking lot, I noticed in the sky a bird, big and flying erratically. Close your eyes and imagine: Home Depot behind us, the main post office over there to the right, Eckerd's to the left, other stores here and there, fifty-five SUVs coming, going all around, and up above, the bird, flying in its peculiar pattern. Suddenly it dropped straight down like a—it wasn't like a rock, it was faster than a rock, more like a bullet, say—and disappeared from view.

There was probably an SUV in the way. So we pulled to a stop behind several of them in the left turn lane there, intending 40th Street, and looked over to the Floyd's Formal Wear and Buckos Dry Cleaning parking lot where stood in the parking space next to a Ford Explosion some kind of small hawk, kite, or kestrel balanced on top of, and with his talons deep inside (it took a few seconds for the brain to focus this picture), some kind of very white victim bird, might've been a pigeon or a dove. Feathers scattered around there. You could see their eyes, the hawk with an irritated stare, for being gawked at, and the dying bird with a sort of bizarrely quiet, uncomprehending look. This is Mississippi, 2003.

The front page of the coast newspaper, the *Sun-Herald*, recently reported the plan for a new Hard Rock Hotel and Casino. It is to be built next door to the Beau Rivage, known locally as "the Beau," a junior cousin to the Bellagio in Las Vegas, opened in 1999 by Steve Wynn's old outfit and currently the fanciest of twelve casinos on the Mississippi coast. One day last month, I pulled out of another casino's parking lot at 5:00 a.m., gazing across the street at a giant Catholic church looming up in the dawning light, wondering what there was to say about Mississippi in 2003, and it came to me. Schizophrenia.

Today the local paper's front page offers a photograph spreading across four of its seven columns. It is a picture of bare-shouldered women, a beautiful white one hugging a beautiful black one who has just become the first African-American to become Mississippi's "Miss Hospitality," and in the background other smiling women. There were tears, too. It's apparently a title of some consequence. I don't make anything of the various participants' apparent joy—their sincerity and insincerity about the same admixture as at the conclusion of all such pageants. In the Miss America competition the first black to be Miss Mississippi won in 1987, sixteen years ago. It's the Sunday newspaper.

The point of these four brief items is only that I don't have to look very hard to find them, and beyond that, that the fabric of life here is as idiosyncratic, rich, painful, incomprehensible, and air-conditioned as anyplace else; but no more so than anyplace else. If you live in some other part of the United States, and the Mississippi that you have in imagination is the clown place drawn in books and (mostly) movies, high and low, well, that's okay, and we hope y'all enjoy it. Just don't come down here looking for it.

Apologies to Faulkner, but today in Mississippi the past, where everything was race and race was everything, while still not dead, is finally past. This is not to say that the state has become a race-blind paradise, that men and women look at each other indifferent to skin color, or that any transaction takes place between people of different races in which ethnicity doesn't figure, or that in a few sections of the state, notably the Delta region, some of the tawdry habits of a hundred years ago don't remain in force. But, for the majority of the place, black people are finally in the game, and in to stay. Race counts, but only in the same way it does in the other forty-nine states.

So I don't have to begin an essay on Mississippi the way all previous essays on Mississippi begin, with a nervous and puzzling caveat suggesting that the state is an odd, sinister place so baffling that outsiders must be hopelessly ill-equipped to think about it. To wit (Beaulah Ratliff, *The Nation*, 1922), "It is hard, perhaps impossible for a Northerner to understand Mississippi . . ." or (John R. Skates, *The Encyclopedia of Southern History*, 1979), "Mississippi, more even than other southern states, is the victim of a stereotype . . ." or even (V. S. Naipaul, *A Turn in the South*, 1989), "It was my wish, in Mississippi, to consider things from the white point of view, as far as that was possible for me. Someone in New York had told me that it wouldn't be easy." Ms. Ratliff goes on to describe a grotesque culture of whites dominating, disenfranchising, and sometimes lynching blacks; Professor Skates acknowledges, in his professorial way, that the stereotype contains much truth ". . . like most stereotypes"; Naipaul inhabits whatever point of view he chooses, effortlessly, or so it seems. In all three cases, one can understand. All Ratliff and Skates seem to mean is that the place is somehow different. Maybe it was. In the century just past, Mississippi certainly spent an awful lot of time, like an angry stepchild, proclaiming it so.

But it seems to me that the state can be pretty well understood in the light of two facts. Of thirty-four states in existence before the Civil War, Mississippi was by some measures the fifth wealthiest, a center of money, influence, and power; after the Civil War, and up to the present day, it has been about the poorest, a stubbornly rural place with a primitive agricultural economy. The second key notion is the racial make-up of the population: for a hundred years, between 1840 and 1940, blacks were the majority—sixty percent of the people—in some counties outnumbering their former masters six or seven to one. As the whites were doing the counting, these numbers probably under-represent the tilt. This doesn't excuse but it does make easier to comprehend the fierce and often criminal anxiety the white population felt. In ways that ranged from polite to barbaric and often twisting themselves into shapes verging on the schizophrenic in the process, Mississippi whites spent a hundred years preventing black citizens from being citizens. Since about 1970, that has faded. But the place is still poor.

To understand Mississippi, the first thing you might do is sit down to watch a dozen or so of the movies made in or about Mississippi in the past fifty years—*Mississippi Burning, This Property is Condemned, A Time to Kill, Crimes of the Heart*—awash with screen doors, oily fat boys with their shirttails hanging out, hysterical women, extra-scrawny dogs, pickups, petticoats, shacks, dirt roads, and deppity sheriffs, buildings of all sorts with startlingly white columns out front, and oceans of y'alls and yessums. It might be set in the eighties or nineties, but everything looks like the fifties or forties. The state stands before you on the steps of the "co't-house," hitching up its ill-fitting pants, wiping its massive brow with a white linen handkerchief. Spittin', maybe.

Well, we're selling y'all that. That clown state that you have heard and seen so much of is our marketing concept. We seem to be able to sell almost boundless amounts of that stuff, your appetite unlimited. You'll buy it in magazine articles, cable

TV specials, on NPR and PBS, in novels and in films, super-charged by Hollywood, as if the place were nothing more than a 48,000-square-mile Seashell & Curio Shoppe. But even in the spots where Mississippians have turned their towns into quaint little caricatures of what the rest of the country thinks of them—the red brick, white column square of Oxford, where the University of Mississippi resides, complete with its own knock-off *Louisiana Hayride* radio show, staffed (apparently) by university students—it's now done with an entirely different sort of self-consciousness than that present in 1936, when the school changed its football team's name to "Rebels." Back then they were probably serious. Previously the nickname had been the Ole Miss "Flood." Nowadays this sort of self-definition is done with circumspection; they know it's a joke. They just don't know how small a joke it is, or how much they are trapped in it.

Because the rest of the country doesn't want to hear anything else from Mississippi. If a laptop and an Escalade and a copy of *USA Today* were to rudely thrust themselves into one of those movies they're always making out of John Grisham or Willie Morris books, bang! There goes the box office. "The image," Noel Polk writes, in his memoir *Outside the Southern Myth*, "can't seem to adjust itself to the reality, no matter how hard it tries," although outside of Polk's own book, it never seems to try very hard.

Meanwhile, after being kept out for more than a hundred years, today black students fill Mississippi classrooms. Much is made of the rise of private white academies, but in one recent year eighty-five percent of the state's white students were in the public schools. Integration is the rule, up to and including the big state colleges where the University of Southern Mississippi's undergraduate enrollment is twenty-one percent African-American, Mississippi State is at sixteen percent, and even Ole Miss, where forty years ago James Meredith's matriculation led white folks to riot, has a black enrollment of about eleven percent. One might note the University of Texas (four percent), UCLA or Berkeley (five percent apiece) or NYU (eight percent). Mississippi has more black elected officials than any other state, and is second only to Georgia for African-American representatives in the U. S. Congress and state legislature, according to the Statistical Abstract of the United States. Mayors, local officials, and education board members are black men and women, as are a fair number of police and those deputy sheriffs the movies are so fond of. Interracial couples, while not common, cause no stir strolling through Wal-Mart.

All this doesn't make it paradise but it is remarkable in a state whose one idea between about 1865 and 1965 was to keep the black population in the agricultural labor force and out of the body politic, a goal implemented in large measure by preventing them from getting an education, and often achieved by violence and the threat of violence. It was, of course, a hundred-year hysteria, and tragic. The strategy was hatched in the Reconstruction period (later, in the South generally, called "the Mississippi Plan"), codified in the Constitution of 1890, and then helped along by Mississippi progressives like the "White Chief," James K. Vardaman, and Theodore Bilbo, who used racial fears as a ticket to power and then used their authority to break the hold of conservative "Bourbon" planters who had run the state before them. Once elected, Vardaman and Bilbo often pursued humane policies regarding prison reform, poor whites, child labor, usury laws, reining in the excesses of corporations and railroads, combining bigotry with progressivism.

The progressive impulse, exemplified in modern times by governors William Winter (1980–84) and Ray Mabus (1988–92), goes back at least to those fans of Andrew Jackson, frontiersmen and small farmers, who settled much of the eastern half of the state, opposed the planter aristocracy that owned the western half, and in the 1820s had sufficient strength to force the capital to be moved from Natchez to its present site, which they renamed Jackson. Historians suggest that had not race been such an issue, this struggle between West and East Mississippi, conservative planters versus Jacksonian poor whites, would have defined the state's politics.

For about twenty years at the beginning of the last century, Vardaman grew into an effective progressive leader. His political career ended in the US Senate when his opposition to the nation's entry into World War I lost him cred back home. We like our wars in Mississippi, always have. Agrarian progressivism also had the unfortunate side effect of reinforcing the white citizens' anti-industrial attitudes about urban and rural life. Vardaman, 1907, quoted in William F. Holmes' biography: "I thank God that we have not great cities. I thank God that we have very few multimillionaires . . ." We still don't have great cities, and the multimillionaires are minus one, now that Bernie Ebbers went down.

But for a hundred years, race trumped everything. The one hysterical idea—the elaborate and obsessive exclusion of the black population from the society around them—that white Mississippians embraced and Vardaman, Bilbo, and others nourished, required of the white population a self-selected isolation from the rest of the nation, an insularity that turned out to be nothing short of economically disastrous. That isolation as much as the suppression of their black brothers and sisters is what white Mississippians have slowly relinquished since the Civil Rights era.

But although race was a major reason for the state's alienation, and federal force the principal reason behind its relinquishing the Neanderthal treatment of its black population, Mississippi's return to the national community has been accomplished by commercial and economic means as well, midwifed by television. Broadcast reporting played a large role in the successes of the Civil Rights Movement, exposing abuses to the rest of the country and to the world. At about the same time, television started showing the rest of the world and its wonders to more and more Mississippians, who, happily or unhappily, likely began craving those bottles of Pepsi-Cola and boxes of Tide and chrome-bejeweled Lincolns and Beatles' records and Swanson TV dinners, just like the citizens of all the other states. The stick and the carrot, delivered by TV. Somehow the old "That's not the way we do it in Miss-re-sippi" didn't cut it anymore.

And so, smacked by the federal stick and lured by luridly advertised sixties consumer goods, Mississippi finally relented to allow its black citizens to be citizens. Very late, the twentieth century sort of roared into Mississippi, ready to make money (overlooking, I suspect, in a great many cases that a great many Mississippians don't have much money).

Nonetheless, down here nowadays, while we still talk funny, just like you we go to the Eckerds and the Rite-Aid and the Walgreens, and that's just for drugstores. There's a Home Depot over there and an Office Depot over that way, past the Gateway store, and down there, a sad little Baskin-Robbins. On the cable we're watching the Weather Channel and HBO and that Republican in drag shouting on *Hardball*. We microwave the bejesus out of practically everything, when we aren't eating Whoppers, Nachos Supreme, or Happy Meals. We buy more Toyotas than an Afghan warlord and SUVs by the truckload, lard up classrooms with computers shipped in by FedEx, with the same magical belief that the machines are surely so fancy they'll educate somebody. We've spent the last few years obsessed with and then forgetting (in order) O. J., Monica and Bill, Kosovo, Gary Condit, Florida, Osama, and Rummy, just like we were supposed to. You bet. We fret about Kobe and WMDs and J. Lo. We hate ourselves while we do it. We're just like you.

Except we probably gamble more. It's our second largest industry. Biloxi, Gulfport, and the other coast towns have been more or less taken over by casinos with their hotels a dozen stories taller than anything else on the skyline, had there been a skyline prior to the casinos' arrival, which there wasn't. Other casinos grace Natchez and Vicksburg, better known for cotton and battlefields, and the biggest development in the state is the campus of casinos in Tunica County, in the Delta, below Memphis. In all, about thirty state casinos make $2.5 billion in revenue and pay $280 million worth of taxes (1999). One might think this would make some huge difference, but other than the new neon skyline, a lot of jobs, increased tourism and tax money, an explosion of pawn shops and payday loan storefronts, and likely a local uptick within the nationwide uptick in bankruptcy filings, major effects haven't yet become visible. No doubt the absentee corporations that own most of the casinos are buying generous chunks of the state and local governments and a sprinkling of judges with campaign cash. Still, the clown Mississippi that exists in the cultural discussion doesn't sort well as the third largest gambling spot in the country. There's history there, too: gambling boats were putting out of Gulfport or Biloxi well before 1991, and a hundred years before that, in 1886, Natchez was first electrified because the casino needed lights.

What I know best of Mississippi are the people who pass through my classes, bearing no resemblance to the clowns in the movies. They are as complicated and mysterious and decent and often wonderful as any strangers anywhere. Oreathia, intense, obsessive, who wanted to make movies even though her father, a musician, wanted her to do something more practical. Diana, the Vicksburg daughter of generations of schoolteachers, who could write like an angel but took up photography; I suspect someday she'll wander back to the typewriter. Bradford, crazy for Kafka (in the German), probably the only student ever to get me to lose my temper in the middle of a class. Rose, forty-five or thereabouts, poorly schooled but thoughtful and acute in her quietly astonishing way, who thinks she can write books, and, given the considerable luck every writer needs and some time, probably can. And Woody, small town Mississippi kid who has about him a strange and sublime seriousness, taking his time, figuring out what he wants to do. On the first of the dozen recommendations I have cobbled up for him over the years, I finally gave up and wrote, "He's sort of like Gandhi." Three white, two black, none quaint. There have been many others.

I don't mean to suggest that it's all enlightenment and racial harmony and shopping malls and cyberculture down here. We have had a very long way to come. It ain't Vienna. Some nights there's junk on the parking lot—usually fried chicken bones, diapers. We've got wall-to-wall Wal-Marts. We have more churches than you have. And Mississippi still has plenty of mean little towns around. But, you know, I was in Carlisle, Pennsylvania, once, if you want to talk mean little towns. Still, we're not urbane. Hattiesburg is the third biggest "city" in Mississippi, with fifty thousand people. Open a Chili's or an Applebee's and you'll make money, but open an interesting restaurant and you'll probably go broke. But, there again, my favorite Austin restaurants were always going under, when I lived in Austin. Once a couple of prospective graduate students from New York and Florida (as best I recall) came here together to look the place over and reported that they had been driving down a street somewhere across town and almost ran over a chicken. Chickens! They were horrified and, of course, delighted. You can still find that clown place or something like it if you're intent on it. Lots of extra-scrawny dogs. Make offer.

Louisiana, Home of the Blues

During the thirty years I lived in neighboring states, I heard only a little about Louisiana, mostly folklore stuff like that was where you hired a first-rate professional killer, or where the roads destroyed your suspension, or where Mardi Gras destroyed your brain cells, or where Cajun food destroyed your stomach lining (but what a way to go, etc.).

I never took time to notice that all of these observations, except maybe about the roads, really only related to that part of Louisiana which dominates, for good and ill, their public relations, the southeastern Creole region (the hit man supposedly was Cajun). When my thoughts wandered over to Louisiana at all, I assumed more or less what Ben Johnson in *The Wild Bunch* says about Mexico, as he gazes across the Rio Grande: "Just looks like more a Texas far's I'm concerned." So, living in the East a few years ago, when I got a teaching job in Louisiana, I was ecstatic. I was going home! Only I wasn't.

Having lived over the years in nine or ten cities in eight states, I have noticed that most places feel just about the same, once you fine tune. In Baltimore, order "chili" and you get sloppy-Joe mix. In Houston, forget about getting a decent cheesesteak. In Mississippi, men are supposed to stare at women (lightly, lightly); in Maryland, they're not. Saying "Howdy!"—or even "Hello!" with an exclamation point—is ill-advised anywhere north of Chatta-nooga. Boston, Denver, even California—all the same, after you learn the local tics. We're all in it together. But Louisiana? No.

The Pelican State is strange. While most Louisianans use the same currency, calendar, and language as natives of the other forty-nine states, in many ways they're about as familiar as Aztecs. The land, the cities, and the attitudes are enough to make a Texan, or any other outsider, feel he's in Tenochtitlan.

The place is beautiful. Driving from Lafayette to Baton Rouge, you ride twenty miles of highway with nothing on either side of the pavement but twenty miles of cypress trees with their roots and considerable trunk under water. Atchafalaya. It's a swamp, but it's a beautiful swamp—which well describes Louisiana as a whole.

In cypress swamps and along the rivers and bayous that cover the state, lush plants and trees seem to assert a power which nature shows only in special parts of other places—Okefenokee, Big Bend, the Everglades.

In Louisiana, your backyard, without care or cultivation, turns into a jungle in a month or two. It's the only place I have ever known where St. Augustine grass could grow to threatening proportions. Don't try to grow things in pots; house plants have mediocre lives here. But should you inadvertently drop something outside on the ground—presto: Brazil. Physically it's beautiful; but the real differences between this state and the other forty-nine are psychological. Louisiana got the blues.

The blues come in a couple of subspecies. Louisiana is really two states, maybe three, depending on how you count New Orleans. I know little about New Orleans, and much has been written about it by others, and anyway, New Orleans is only technically in Louisiana, about the way Hong Kong is in China or Oz is in Kansas. It's a place to itself. The rest divides in two.

Louisiana One, the southern/southeastern part, familiar to many people by virtue of the aforementioned public relations, is a pleasantly decadent, if dangerous, region, largely Catholic, heavily Cajun-French. The whole state is a land of despair, but in the south it's an extremely good-natured despair.

People from the south and southeast know how to feel hopeless in a carefree sort of way that only Catholics seem to master. They party hardy and eat boudin and crawfish (it's work), the bars stay open all night, the jokes are endless and sometimes enhanced by Cajun dialect which takes a while to catch on to. They know how to sin, but they've forgotten how to worry about it. Nobody worries too much about anything, I suppose because everyone has known from an early age that he is damned.

Southern Louisianans identify with Houston—the Astros, the Rockets, the Galleria—sports and shopping; otherwise, they consider the rest of the world irrelevant. How else explain one readable newspaper (Baton Rouge's) in a state of four and a half million people? If New Yorkers think they are the center of the universe, and Texans wish they were the center, Louisianans are content. Their state isn't in the universe.

—

If you drive north on Highway 165 from Lake Charles, four hours later you arrive in the city of Monroe, exhausted. The north-south highways in Louisiana live up to their reputation. Even riding the big Interstates 10 and 20 east and west, you tend to pray your ball joints hold up till you hit Texas or Mississippi pavement. But the north-south highways are two-lane blacktop, and if you come up on a haywagon or a truck loaded with huge yellow pine logs, well, relax and enjoy it.

Monroe, like Shreveport and Alexandria, is Louisiana Two, which comprises all of north and most of central and west Louisiana. In other words, most of the state—the Louisiana one never hears about. Here they identify with Dallas—the Rangers, the Mavericks, the Trade Mart. Monroe and West Monroe, politically distinct but separated only by the Ouachita ("Wash-i-taw") River, have a combined population of about eighty thousand. A small city, with levees and freeways, advertising agencies and an art museum, a zoo, a ten-thousand-student university.

Trucks cruise the streets spraying into the air a mist of what smells like Malathion—there's a slight mosquito problem, you see. The house I moved into had long gooey yellow strips of paper hanging beside both doors—there's a tiny fly problem. There are few storm sewers, only ditches, so when it rains (and it rains a lot) your lawn becomes a pool. Periodically a prison gang of black men appears and digs the ditches deeper, shepherded by a fat, white overseer, who sits under a tree. We're talking Otto Preminger movie.

Louisiana is almost thirty percent black, and the race relations here are a revelation. The prejudice toward and suffering of the black population are very real, and much as they have been described in newspapers and books and movies for the past thirty years. But there's something else, something which I never came across anywhere else, either in media reports or in day to day life.

You see in Louisiana a kind of integration which doesn't show up in the national press and which doesn't exist in Northern cities or in Texas or Mississippi. It is not only that black and white children play together, or black and white workers ride in the same pickup truck, or black and white students share classrooms and homework. It's the easy, natural way they do it. The racial hostility may eclipse anything in those other places, but it's more complicated than that. Blacks and whites know each other better here.

At least, this is how I have come to understand whites who in the afternoon sometimes entertain a carload of black friends, and some nights are out on the street yelling "Niggers!" at the top of their lungs, over some real or imagined crime or slight. Even bigotry is not simple.

The situation has its less serious aspects, too, like the fact that whites' dogs bark at blacks and blacks' dogs bark at whites. Some neighborhoods are integrated (which makes for a God Almighty lot of barking), but most are not. If you are white, your neighbors will most likely be white.

Your neighbors. They dress in camouflage gear (it's not a joke) and carry fishing rods, and sometimes rifles, in and out of the house all day, but they are neighborly in the extreme, expressed mostly in gifts of food and long conversations about the governor, which take place in the front yard.

The governor, for anyone who has not heard, was twice indicted (one mistrial and one acquittal; had to do with nudging some money into the side pocket) and is viewed by most of his subjects as something between a lovable rogue and a clumsy gambler. At one trial it came out that he had lost around $500,000 in Reno, but Governor Edwards allowed as how he had actually won more than $500,000 as well, which was presented as evidence that he didn't need some millions worth of tainted money, but we all figured what he really wanted was to salvage his pride. No one in Louisiana wants to be thought of as a clumsy gambler. After a brief retirement enforced by the voters, the same voters brought him back. Between the two trials, the governor offered his solution to the state's oil-poisoned economy: a statewide lottery, and casinos for New Orleans. Courage, some might say gall, not often found in governors of other states, who look a little freeze-dried compared to Edwin Edwards.

You can have other neighbors (who also talk about the governor, in less forgiving terms) if you want to live in the yuppie ghetto, which is small, and, I'm afraid, populated mostly by Texans, who for some reason can't go home. Outside this little enclave, the word "yuppie" is meaningless here. Which is a certain kind of good fortune, I suppose.

Besides mosquitoes and flies and camouflage clothing, what Monroe has a lot of is police. If when you are struck by a car in Austin, there's a fifty-fifty chance it'll be a Saab, in Monroe it's fifty-fifty a police car. In classes, a fair number of my best students were cops. Others, who disappeared for a couple weeks a semester, were cops of a different sort; they arrived with a note from the dean and the explanation that they'd been in Honduras. In any case, police and military visions have a hold on the popular imagination. When you go to see *Rambo*, no one laughs.

—

In northern Louisiana, as in the southern part of the state, the prevailing wind carries with it the despair of people who live an insular existence, who don't expect to "make it," who are plenty satisfied with what is, and don't lose much time comparing what is in their neck of the swamp with what is anywhere else. The media-dominated life which people live in other places doesn't signify.

The difference, in northern Louisiana, is that despair and complacency do not make the people charming, or happy. The local newspaper writes headlines like "Leaving Up to His Name," can't spell, banners silly stories about paving plans and social events. In Texas, someone would buy it, or start another newspaper. Not so Louisiana.

You notice it on the faces of Kmart checkers, and waitresses in restaurants, and students, and businessmen in three piece suits, even sometimes in the eyes of the actors in local TV commercials. If the water is full of chemical garbage, what's the difference? If the newspaper is shabby and illiterate, who cares? If the streets are pocked and littered with trash, so what? If the air stinks, it's the paper mill. Don't worry about it.

Monroe. At one corner of a tiny, decrepit used car lot a gray, weatherbeaten forties Chevy or Buick hangs twenty feet in the air. Across town, on the way to the A&P, at the front of a combination storage units-motel operation is a brightly lit glassed-in room into which has been stuffed, shining, an old white Lincoln Continental. On the other side of the street a huge dead oak tree used to stand with cut limbs on which hung sixty or seventy old automobile tires. Someone, maybe the wind, knocked it down. Too bad. Used to be, if you were at loose ends with nothing to do on a Friday night, you could always go out and look at the tire tree.

Boredom is endemic, but there's always the Louisiana Purchase Gardens and Zoo. Monroe has a wonderful zoo; if you go, make sure you get the right entrance road, because next to the tourist road is another which takes you to a park in which every face is young, hostile and bored, and checks you out for that DEA look. If you aren't selling or buying, you aren't welcome.

Along with the zoo and the mosquito-fogging trucks are fern bars which look like cafeterias, pleasant bars which are empty, monster trucks instead of Hondas, and newsstands clogged with *Gung Ho* and *Soldier of Fortune* in place of *Runner's World* and *Vanity Fair*. As if the past thirty years hadn't happened. At any moment you expect to see drinking fountains marked "White" and "Colored." Which is interesting because while the white Louisianan is resigned to despair, his black brother and sister are more hopeful. At least some are. Some of the young black Louisianans believe in the TV world, the magazine world, the Michael Jordan and Arsenio and Snoop Dogg world, and believe that's where they are headed.

I hope they are right. Someone else can tell them what is spiritually correct to want, and what isn't. After two years in Louisiana, the sight of people who want anything more than what they've got is a welcome one.

It may best tell what most of Louisiana is like, that the nearest thing to a familiar image, and the one that stands out from two years of impressions, is the image of a few black college kids who smile, and laugh, and dream big, who for all the world look like the white Sigma Nus and Kappa Sigs, Pi Phis and Tri Delts I remember from other times and other places, who if they think about tomorrow at all think it will be better than today. They are a minority of a minority; most of their brothers and sisters, sitting on the porches of shotgun houses, have quit dreaming. Like most everyone else in Louisiana.

Urban Farmer, Amiable Crop

It's only natural. The urban farmer first heads to the lumberyard and picks up twelve feet of 1" x 8" and eight feet of 1" x 12", and of course some 1" x 2" for runners so the roof won't rot. What is the urban farmer doing? He's building a planter, in which he will grow his own tomatoes.

His attitude toward the project is complex, but not very interesting. The dispute with Sartre. The garden hose in myth and metaphor. That sort of thing. It distills to the fact that tomatoes run to $1.29 the pound, and the other fact that everyone on his block is growing them. Clearly, it's his sort of fad.

—

Home with his twelve dollars' worth of lumber, he borrows some power tools and engages a friend in building the planter. The friend nails crudely, but fast. It takes an afternoon. Completed, the planter box is so handsome that the urban farmer briefly considers using it as bookshelves, or a boat. As night settles over the little city, he is sitting in the planter on the roof, smoking. Then he gets out, remembering tobacco mosaic, a plant disease he has read about.

As any dilettante farmer can tell you, reading about growing things is a mistake. But the urban farmer insists. Days later he staggers out to his planter (staggers up, actually, because it's on the roof). He is not now thinking of the beautiful blond wood. He is thinking of fusarium wilt, blossom end rot, nematodes, sunscald, leafminers, leaf hoppers, hornworms, and aphid-herding ants.

Luckily (as they always say in plant books) he has been excessively cerebral since childhood and knows just what to do in such a situation. Press on regardless. Dirt! he thinks. But first, prepare for the dirt with a layer of rocks on the bottom for drainage. Drainage is very important, as in life.

Now, as Freud taught us, there are always problems if you know how to look for them. The urban farmer quickly invents two (suppressing the initial hypochondria; dirty rocks). First, how large should the rocks be? And second, where does one secure a good wheelbarrow load of rocks? Reading in his tomato book reveals that its author thinks carelessly. Size is not specified.

Down the block is a driveway with a good number of rocks just lying around. The driveway has been abandoned, and leads to nothing. He drives down to the driveway and parks, gets out with an old pillowcase and looks around. Sees himself, briefly, in a newspaper photograph, up on three hundred and twelve counts of rock theft. Loud, Vulgar, A Neighbor Recalls.

A half hour later, on the roof with the rocks, he pours them into his planter, picking out the sticks, slivers of green glass, pop tops, and other assorted garbage. Size no longer matters. He is pressing on regardless.

Dirt is obtained in much the same manner. In exactly the same manner, in fact, with a lot of speculation about pH, humus, clay, sand, and microorganism content. What exactly is humus? he wonders. The speculation is blessedly idle. Dirt is dirt, as the saying goes. He mixes in sand borrowed from the landlord, and as a sweetener, a couple of bags of "pasteurized" potting soil. The soil costs four dollars.

Resting, he tries to figure out the difference between filth that will grow twenty-three foot plants (pictured in the text) and filth which needs pasteurizing. Between good and bad filth. This is the sort of question which always arises when he attempts to explore environmental ideology.

The question is too much. He contents himself with facts. Horse, rabbit, and sheep manures are hot manures (rich in nitrogen), cow and hog are cold. Cat manure, readily available, is not covered.

The urban farmer has now spent eight days and sixteen dollars and feels ready. He buys three plants and sets them in the planter, burying them up to their chins, as the books instruct. Not to miss any bets, he speaks warmly to his plants, when no one else is around—you never know when talk show trivia is going to pay off. After some early hesitation, the plants begin growing. It is a miracle of course, and he is suitably awed. Just like a power drill! he thinks. It works!

—

From here the process accelerates. Miracle is piled on miracle. Buds appear, then blossoms, small and yellow, then tiny green tomatoes. To avoid being too natural, the urban farmer runs out and buys, for two dollars, a jar of greenish crystals which when flooded with water become a chemical fertilizer. This he lavishes on his plants. They appear to love it. They appear to love it because they stand straight up and raise their limbs. But, they may be shrieking, who can tell?

Then, just as the lore has it, aphids appear, herded by ants. The herding itself is difficult to see. The ants may be just hanging around. The aphids are fat, translucent, and reddish. Blood of my plants, the urban farmer thinks. His book comes in very handy at this point, lapsing into technology.

It suggests putting aluminum foil under the plants because the aphids, on the underside of the leaves, can't stand the reflected sunlight. This he understands perfectly and does immediately.

Results are inconclusive. He assumes the aphids are going crazy, because he has a good attitude.

More tomatoes appear, all of them growing larger by the day. They are all green. When will they turn red? The urban farmer makes his second mistake by calling three experts at three local plant shops. The experts are in a three-way disagreement over how long it takes for the tomatoes to ripen. The sort of advice one gets for free.

He is saved by yet another miracle. One by one, a day or two at a time, the tomatoes turn red. They are huge by this point. They taste, as advertised, markedly better than the ones he is used to. The plants likely have catface, cutworms and psyllid yellows, but are plugging onward, manufacturing tomatoes. A week or so more and there are dozens of them. This must be what it feels like to be rich.

He attempts to give two particularly fine specimens to his neighbor, but she declines, having a degree in horticulture and a few plants of her own. He attempts to give them to the landlord, the postman, the butcher, and a golden retriever. They are all harvesting their own. He sits in a comfortable chair at a modest little desk in his apartment with forty pounds of ripe tomatoes overhead, experiencing that most shattering of all experiences. Success.

An Old Acquaintance

I spent my childhood in the fields and bayous far out on the west side of the city, in an area which in the years since has been overrun with high-rise steel and plate glass. A good Southern boy, I had a natural affinity for and acquaintance with animals of all kinds, but especially with reptiles. A neighborhood friend and I collected hundreds of snakes, from the locally abundant hognose snakes to exotics collected by mail-order like South American anacondas and a Cook's tree boa. They were as much pets as any Cocker Spaniel, with pet names and special favorites and elaborate mourning when they died, which they did not infrequently.

Each summer on the screen porch of his parents' house we would create a "zoo" consisting of twenty or thirty snakes as well as his dog, my dog, crickets, tarantulas, caterpillars, lizards, turtles, and whatever other fauna we had come across that year. When not down at the bayou or in the woods hunting more, we were caring for our collection, gathering food—in a pinch, zoo inhabitants were sometimes fed to other zoo inhabitants—keeping records, and sometimes watching over snake eggs until they hatched.

Then I got older. He went off to Sewanee, I went to the University of Texas. Years passed. I lost friends, attitudes, hair. But, oddly, the childhood affinity for animals never went away.

Sometime after college, still living in Austin, while mowing a friend's yard for her, I happened on a clutch of a dozen snake eggs, hidden under a stone. I figured she didn't want them, so I took them home and prepared a nest of paper towels and kept watch for six weeks. Eleven hatched, to be released later in a wooded area near Lake Austin.

This persistence of herpetological interests into adulthood might have seemed strange, but I discovered it wasn't only me. Once, much later, my friend and fellow zookeeper from childhood saw something I had written and telephoned me, and the next time I was back in my hometown I went over to see him. A glance at the handsome, sprawling new house in a fashionable neighborhood told me that in the twenty years since I had last seen him he had become a millionaire. A green Jaguar was parked out front.

Inside, we sat and talked a bit and he showed off his handsome children. We drank Cokes, like we had thirty years earlier on the porch of his parents' house, and talked about my career, his thriving business, people we'd known. Then we got down to cases, and went upstairs to look over a snake collection, which he tried, indifferently, to pass off as his son's.

Later, after I moved to Monroe, Louisiana, to take a teaching job, my wife and I got into the habit of taking walks in the desolate fields behind the football stadium. A tiny stream ran across one of the fields. Resurrecting an old habit, I would walk in the reeds along the stream, staring down. We caught jittery and illtempered garter snakes, which my wife decided she didn't like when one of them bit me. Then one June day we found Horace.

About fourteen inches long, a deep brown with a black stripe running along low on each side of his slender body, Horace was a Gulf salt marsh snake. Not at all like the jittery, biting garter snakes; Horace would curl up on your palm and go to sleep. At least that's what my wife told me he was doing. Because snakes have no eyelids, their eyes never close, so their sleep is hard to call.

We took him home and made him a place in the bathtub, until I could get a cage or an aquarium for him to live in. One night my wife came into the little office I had made out of the extra bedroom and said, "Horace is gone." And sure enough the bathtub was empty. My wife was a good sport, but you could tell that his undetermined whereabouts made her just the least bit anxious.

One morning about a week later, stepping out the front door, I looked down into the front garden and there was Horace crawling happily along the front wall. We got an aquarium with no further delay. After that, things went along fine until August when I got a new and better teaching job in Mississippi.

We packed in a hurry, drove back and forth between Monroe and Hattiesburg house hunting, said goodbye to the good friends we had made in Louisiana, all the wearying and wrenching rituals of moving. The last ritual was to take Horace back out to the little clear stream where we had found him.

We looked for a spot with plenty of minnows and grass high enough to hide in. When we persuaded him out of the big mayonnaise jar and into the clear water, he stopped for a minute, as if trying to remember this. Then suddenly he was all *s*'s and dove to the bottom, a distance of about six inches, and then after another moment we saw his head rise slightly above the surface of the water a little further on, as if now he was looking back, saying goodbye. We appreciated that.

Gamblers

(with Frederick Barthelme)

It was not exactly that we liked our fellow gamblers, the dealers, the pit and floor people, the cocktail waitresses. It was more that we loved them, at a respectable distance, the same distance at which one loves characters in books or on television shows. Some of them were interesting and some were funny and some were pretty. The gamblers were surprisingly good-natured, on the whole, with a few rude or angry exceptions, and those few served by their very failings to point out what good fellows the rest of our companions were and what a good time we were all having.

One night a Hispanic couple came to an already crowded blackjack table where we were playing, the woman taking the last chair and the man standing beside and behind her, whispering urgent instructions in Spanish. Sometimes she would argue. She was sort of gorgeous. She bet her two green chips—fifty dollars—and won the first hand. She bet her now four greens and won the second hand, doubling her money again. She parleyed the two hundred into four, four into eight. By this point everyone else around the table, including us, was participating in her good fortune.

In fact, the other players at the table were now in a sort of ecstasy, like in a basketball game when someone on your team strokes a shot from half court. Not that anybody said anything, mind you. It was a tiny look, a glance, a smile. The woman, who might have been Cuban, had stopped betting her whole stake on every hand, but she was still betting heavily, and mostly she was winning. She may have lost a couple of hands.

Soon—it couldn't have been more than ten or fifteen minutes—she had turned her fifty dollars into two thousand, all in green chips in front of her at the rim of the table. No one announced that, and no one stared. People typically stack chips in recognizably sized stacks, and after a while you can reckon in a glance. Two thousand dollars is ten stacks of green, eight chips high, two hundred dollars in each, or maybe two one-thousand-dollar ten-high stacks of blacks.

By this point a transformation had come over the rest of the players at the table. There we all sat, some of us sharing, in a minor way, in her winning streak, but all of us participating vicariously. It was exactly what we had all come to the casino for, this miraculous multiplication wherein fifty dollars becomes two thousand, wherein your risk returns forty-fold. If you sit in a casino at a gaming table or at a slot machine for any period of time, some stranger will always say, "Some woman hit that one there for two grand last night. Then she hit it again for two more, five minutes later," or, "Aren't you the guy who won five thousand on three-card poker?" If you're a regular player, among the dozens of times you've gone home thousands in the hole, maybe once or twice, you were the guy.

But something else was going on at about the point the Cuban woman and her boyfriend topped two thousand. The ecstasy was drying up. There were six people sitting at the table: us, the woman, a forty-something mother and her twenty-something daughter, and a young black guy wearing a leather hat. There we all were, swallowing. We all had the same thought, pretty much at the same moment. You could see us straining, trying to communicate telepathically: Run. Take the money. Get it out of the casino.

There was perhaps a brief moment's hesitation, a pause, in which the boyfriend and the beauty stared at the stacks that had miraculously appeared in front of them, as if wondering what they should do, as if there really were a possibility that they might scoop them up and hustle them over to one of the cashiers behind the long counter and take their money and run. But of course, that did not happen.

What happened was what everybody at the table knew was going to happen—even the Cuban couple themselves, we suspect—which we knew because we had done it two dozen, four dozen times ourselves. They gave the money back; they bet it, bit by bit, until the eighty green chips were all back in the rack in front of the dealer. She frowned at him, he looked at her and shrugged, and then she gave a tiny laugh and slipped off her chair, and they disappeared.

Another time, we were playing on one-dollar video poker machines with a Vietnamese guy and a chubby, middle-aged white woman. We were sitting in the middle of the row of machines, with the Vietnamese guy and the woman on either side of us. They had been there before us and apparently had struck up an acquaintance as they were now cajoling their machines and talking to each other over our heads about the hands they were getting, and sometimes the woman would call the guy down to see what she had gotten, or maybe to advise on a draw. It was clear somehow that they had just met. One forms brief but intense relationships with utter strangers while gambling together, which is as intoxicating and as intimate as drinking together, although as a rule, less messy.

Sometime during that half hour, as we punched the buttons on the machines, our fortunes bouncing up and down in gentle swings, Steve placed a new bet and turned up a new hand: the ace, ten, jack, and queen, all hearts, and the seven of clubs. Four cards of a royal straight flush, on a video poker machine the best possible hand, the perfect conclusion. With the "hold" buttons above the four royal hearts each carefully pushed and carefully checked, we both looked at the seven about to be discarded. "King," Rick said, and when Steve pushed the "draw" button the seven flashed away and the King of hearts appeared. All five of them.

The Vietnamese guy, whom we had forgotten about, knew instantly. "Royal flush," he said, in the way one might say, "It's a girl!" or "He's alive!" He looked from us to the screen, and back again. The screen itself was pretty excited, flashing the cards of the royal flush on and off in some sequence of its own devising. "Let me tell her," the guy said. He pointed to the woman. It wasn't, "Please let me tell her." It was, "Stop. Don't do a thing until I tell her." He waved for her attention, told her what had happened right beside her, on a machine she herself had probably been playing ten minutes earlier. The big woman gave a slight smile, sighed, and then returned to her own poker machine more fiercely committed than ever.

The win was two hundred and fifty dollars; if the original bet had been five coins instead of one, it would have been four thousand. But that wasn't the point. Here was one reason gambling was so seductive, even though we almost always ended up losing. The perfect thing had happened. Here was something most of our friends and colleagues at the university either did not know or no longer believed in. They had grown up, become wise, accepted things as they were. But everybody in the casino knew. However strange, however crude, however self-deluded, these people knew how to hope, how to imagine life as something other than a dreary chore. They imagined something wonderful happening. You might change your life. A fool's secret shared by gamblers with drunks, artists, and children, all of which they resemble.

In our day to day lives, practically no one we knew knew much sense of possibility or even seemed capable of imagining possibility, let alone perfection. We worked in an English department, after all, and that was a problem. It was Lucky Jim, watered down by half. What were we to do for conversation? Would we choose the esteemed colleague who pressed his long-time female graduate students to call him "Santa" in his office, but please, please, "Doctor Claus" when speaking to him in the halls, where others might hear? Or maybe the woman who said in a search committee meeting, speaking of a highly qualified job applicant, "Not her. She's too good. She'd never come here." Another was waging a bitter, twenty-year war on student evaluations, while others taught seminars in which long consideration of wrongs done to the clitoris filled the hours. Socially, they were pleasant, and we liked them. It was just a little hard to participate in the things they cared about, which in turn made it hard to have a satisfying conversation.

We better understood the gamblers than these men and women whose dedication near as we could tell was not to scholarship, literature, or students so much as getting on with tenure and promotion, and sounding good in faculty meetings the meanwhile. They did that, they sounded good in the meetings, full of purpose and high sentence. They were genial, intelligent, and not without charm. We had friends among them, mostly in our little bunker of creative writing, but the milieu was sort of suffocating. You saved your jokes for the students, who had enough imagination left to get them, and to make jokes of their own. Jokes themselves, which were the basis of our social training in the family, what there was of it, were suspect in the university, where behaving with an air of seriousness was "privileged," as they say, not knowing that if you have to act serious, likely you aren't. Our fellow gamblers were serious in the furious way children are serious, concentrating on play, oblivious, intense, but at ease. Essentially, they came to the casino to be children.

Gambling is a child's vice practiced largely by adults, and often by the old. Every day sometime after eight in the morning the casinos see clouds of gray-haired folks, in couples and groups, arrive in buses which have brought them from the airport or along the coast from Florida. We were often there to greet them. Many were sixty and seventy. Whatever age, they come to play. Because money is involved, it's play with an extra edge, but it's still play, they are still children. That was something we understood.

We were children. We weren't particularly proud of that, but we weren't ashamed of it either, and we had suffered enough boredom, done enough work, taken enough responsibility, and watched enough hypocrisy to not worry too much about it. Dimly, but often, one begins to notice that a lot of what passes for maturity, wisdom or hard-bitten realism looks like play-acting. Who can't pretend to be John Huston? We preferred his father, an older but younger man.

This may have had something to do with our own father. One of father's most redeeming characteristics was his intense childlike curiosity, even in his eighties. He was a difficult man, and sometimes distant. He liked to think about things, like a child, in a way that foregrounded ideas and gave barely a nod to feelings. He believed that if one just thought well enough, anything could be solved, ameliorated, fixed. By careful reasoning, father felt, anyone could make a rich and happy life, overlooking the fact that it hadn't worked so well for him. I just haven't yet figured it out, he would have said. He would have said he was still working on it. He was always working on something. He tried hard to allow for the disorder emotions introduced into every situation, but his allegiance was with thinking, not feeling, so frequently when father started thinking, someone's delicate feelings got flattened. This caused him no end of trouble with us, with all his family. For father, most situations eventually came down to, Well, it shouldn't be. It isn't reasonable. In his way, he was a kind man, whose kindness took the peculiar form of thinking for you as hard as he could, because thinking was one of the things he was good at.

He had about him, too, other childlike qualities, the intensity, an intolerance for boredom, which he had preserved into adulthood and old age. He cared passionately about things he did, and he was always doing things because, again like a child, he was an optimist and an idealist. The insistent hope, or sense of possibility, the idea that things could be better, could be made better, if you tried hard enough, if you figured well enough, if you got another, better idea, if you just kept at it, was one of his abiding gifts to his sons, who customarily disguised their imbecilic idealism in irony which they weren't imbecilic enough to take seriously.

We knew how to be ironic and cynical, we'd been bathed in it since forever, it was auto-pilot, the default setting, it was what the university people thought "smart" meant, but it was just so tiresome, and there were so many dim people who were fond of it. Not stupid people who didn't know any better, but the smart people, the ones who ran the literature business and the university business, and the TV news and newspapers and the culture and the country in general. They were so disheartening. Why aren't they better? They could be better, we thought. The sort of thought Pop would have.

It was a battle to remember, while we were sitting playing at a blackjack table with some guy with a Massachusetts accent and a twelve-penny common nail the diameter of a small pencil bent in half and hanging from his pierced ear, telling snail jokes, that life was a dreary chore, designed that way by the Good Lord for some inexplicable reason. We preferred the idea of jokes and jackpots, preferred to think that some great new blackjack strategy or more-fabulous-than-ever run of cards would come. Each time in the car rolling down to Gulfport, part of the ritual was "here's the new plan," both serious and not, a hope and a joke. It was a problem, this tendency to think that good things were going to happen, that things would turn out well, in the face of acres of evidence to the contrary. Father could never have anticipated that his faith that things really did make sense and his hope that by just keeping at it success would be won would be half-learned lessons figuring, after his death, in his sons' contributing thousands and thousands of dollars of his painstakingly preserved money to casinos.

In something of this way, we understood the other gamblers, too. They hoped like we hoped, they knew what we knew. They were always talking about what their husbands or wives were going to do to them (a wiry little drunk checks his watch at six in the morning and says, "She's a'ready thrown my clothes in the yard, but tha's a'right. I can change in the yard. Got to be at work at eight, and it's a two-hour drive from here"), but they were always looking for an opportunity to celebrate, their good

fortune or ours, anybody on our team will do. We liked thinking of our fellow gamblers as a team, liked treating money—that
bully—like it was so many Slim Jim paper towels, liked the fact
that people don't lie much while gambling, less than, say, at a
meeting. A community of vice makes hypocrisy unnecessary, so
one doesn't have to listen to it.

If this was true of the gamblers, it was even more true of the
people who worked at the casino, who though they were being
paid to be nice to us, had no reason not to, anyway. We were
nice to them. We liked them. These relationships were similar
to those that everyone strikes up with people who work in their
doctor's office or supermarket, except that we were often at the
casino eight or twelve or twenty-four hours at a time. Sometimes,
after having dealt to us on a Thursday night, finished his shift
and gone home, a dealer would show up fresh on Friday night
and, recognizing us with an almost imperceptible look of shock,
recover, saying, "Not going well, I guess?"

We didn't really know them; we saw them only at the casino.
Still, at that distance, we understood what they said, and they
understood us, which was no small thing. Our relationships with
them were like our relationships with Shane and Jim Rockford
and Kleist and Hamlet and Hakeem Olajuwon, about as super-
ficial and about as dear.

The people we saw all the time weren't management, but dealers and pit and floor personnel, waiters and waitresses, cashiers
and so on. Some had come from Las Vegas or New Jersey, but
many were local people who had had other jobs and other lives
on the Mississippi coast before hiring on to work in the new
casinos. They were making more money now, but they liked this
work better, too.

Dealing blackjack or craps can't be any less dulling and repet-
itive than a lot of other work, and the "glamour" of the casinos is
so thin you could scratch it away with a fingernail. Still, there's
an element of carelessness and chance, instant by instant, card
by card, roll by roll, which you don't find at the department store
or the gas company or the elementary school. And a dealer is a

performer, gets to talk while he or she works, make wise cracks, cluck at you like a chicken when you make some cowardly play, or tell jokes. They would tell us to go home when it was obvious we should, there not being much penalty for telling the truth, nor much likelihood that we would go. They had styles, some surprising—some stubby, prim-looking woman resembling your fourth grade teacher asked by a player if he should split tens, would look at him deadpan and say, "You had a twenty-inch dick, would you cut it in half?"—but the possibility of having a style at all is something most jobs don't much offer.

You got the sense that many of the dealers were people who themselves had a very low tolerance for boredom and the narrow definition of proper behavior required in nine to five jobs they had held before. Some of them were just young and paying their way through college, but for others, working in a casino was a way to flee the dreariness of their previous work as school teachers or sales clerks or secretaries. Here the pay was better, and they got to make jokes, tell the truth, perform, play. That was an impulse we understood. We liked the jokes. We knew the people. They were family.

People's Right to Allegedly, Sort of Know

Toiling away as a college professor, I had begun to suspect that my promised fifteen minutes of fame weren't ever coming, but finally I got lucky. Sort of. Three years ago, I managed to get thrown out of a casino and later charged with a crime, and because my brother Rick, an established novelist, was also charged, this nightmare eventually showed up in the newspapers. It was fourteen minutes, but hey, who's counting?

The charge was cheating. It was alleged that we had conspired with a chubby, likeable young woman who dealt blackjack. We had not conspired; in fact we had lost lots of money. Still, the dream went on and on, a costly tour of the legal system, two years of uneasy sleep. The charges against us were completely dismissed last week, but before that, they were news.

Writing about you, newspapers say what they want, and slant it how they please, leaving you little recourse. You can write a letter to the editor.

A year and some months after the original incident, a reporter from the *New York Times* discovered it and flew down to Mississippi to do a story, later reprinted in a dozen other newspapers. According to the published story, the prosecutors wouldn't talk to him. He talked to Rick, briefly, and not at all to me. He did talk to our employer, our students, and, most cordially, to the casino people. He's the *Times*' gambling writer. He was staying in the casino's hotel.

He wrote, "According to court documents and people involved in the case, the two men were in the casino more than a year ago when surveillance cameras observed them receiving signals from the dealer and being paid for hands they did not win—a practice known as 'dumping the game.'" This last was a mystery; no court document accused us of being paid for hands we did not win.

None of this came from us or the prosecutors, so you can probably figure out who "people involved in the case" are—casino and gaming commission people. What the cameras really "observed" weren't signals, but physical movements, like "dealer nods her head," things that were then interpreted with great gusto. The interpretation was all being done by the casino and the gaming commission people, although the *Times*man omits that fact. "According to people involved in the case," he says.

I knew a little about newspapers. Acquaintances had sometimes shown up in newspaper stories, just usually not in unsavory reports about accusations of crimes. Once long ago in my hometown paper, the *Houston Chronicle*, there was an article about my family and how the five children were all writers.

It was a nothing little piece, but in its way it was quietly astonishing. My brother Donald was called "David" in this story, for instance, and some prize another brother had won for a painting at the Oklahoma City Arts Festival was described as having been won at the "Oklahoma State Fair," suggesting an award for a prize heifer or some grotesquely large pumpkin. The story contained a half dozen other small errors, as well. At the time, we laughed about it.

Of course, it's not only inaccuracies, it's what is today called "spin," the way sentences are written, what's left out and what's left in, and the way things are set next to one another to suggest this or that.

Consider these sentences from a *Boston Globe* story. Their reporter quotes a talkative old friend of ours with whom he had insinuated himself. She had gone gambling with us often. He must have talked to her a long time. His hard work finally got him something to put in the paper, discussing how Rick and I had treated blackjack dealers: "'It wasn't any boyfriend-girlfriend flirtation,' she said. 'It was just their style. They like to make women feel pretty.'" The writer then adds, helpfully: "Steve is married; Rick has a steady woman companion . . ."

A few lines earlier it has been claimed that "it was not unusual for the brothers to strike up friendships with several of the women dealers," which is true as far as it goes, but leaves out that it is not unusual for us—or any regular player at a casino—to strike up friendships with all the dealers, women or men, pretty or homely. The "friendships" here cited don't amount to potential criminal conspiracy, either; "Hey, Steve," they say; "Hey, Brad," you say. "You ever sell your boat?" Maybe they ask where you work; maybe you ask what they did before they became a blackjack dealer. That about covers it.

The *Globe* writer, eager to report our charming ways, chose to omit all this other information that one might think the people have a right to know. The people might misconclude that we were sinister Lotharios out there making women feel pretty all the time. Whatever. Reliable sources suggest the *Boston Globe's* idea of the truth is very liberal, what with their plagiarism problems and so on.

The journalist's self-justifying phrase—"the people's right to know"—sounds smug the second time you hear it, a smugness which gets louder after you yourself have been the subject of some foggy reporting. The *Times* and the *Globe* felt the people had such a pressing need to know about my indictment that they put it on their front pages. Would they put the story of the charges dismissed on page one as well? Nope. In the *Times* it was buried ten or so pages inside; the *Globe* may have reported it, or may have not.

In the *Globe* story I am forty-six years old, in the *Times* forty-nine, both wrong, but I appreciate it. Here is a funny sentence from the *Times* story: "University officials were unaware of the charges against the two professors until today." You know what happened "today," how those poor university officials were brought out of the darkness? The gambling reporter from the *New York Times* called them.

In yet another newspaper the university's PR spokesman was quoted as saying we were owed the presumption of innocence "until the legal process runs its course." Yes, that presumption is an awful nuisance.

Newspaper reporters get around that presumption, and hope to protect themselves from legal actions, with stock adverbs and phrases—"allegedly" and "according to people involved in the case" and so on—which if you're like most people, in fact, if you're like me, you have come to ignore when you read. That's a mistake. In that "allegedly" is the whole other half of any story, the half that the reporter isn't particularly friendly to, or was too lazy to get, or thinks might offend acquaintances of his.

Like most middle-class Americans, I tend to believe what I read in newspapers, even though I know better, even though I know that in every newspaper story about something about which I had firsthand knowledge of the facts, the newspaper got facts wrong. Not some stories; every story. What is far worse, like too many middle-class Americans, if I read in the newspaper that someone is indicted or accused of a crime, I assume they're guilty. At least, before I got my fourteen minutes of fame, I used to.

I Do, I Do

Last December 31 Melanie and I celebrated our first wedding anniversary on our twenty-first New Year's Eve, after one year of marriage and twenty years of living together. Call us cautious.

I don't ever remember myself making, back in the seventies, those popular remarks about marriage being "just a piece of paper," the denial then of a difference between "living in sin"—cohabitation—and marrying. That quarrel seemed a part of some other world, not mine. I do recall the rapacious joy with which married friends avidly greeted the news that cohabitants they knew were getting married, as if their doubt about their own marrying was salved by friends' caving in and doing the conventional thing, too. And I remember feeling I was just as committed to my girlfriend as they were to their wives. Many of them, of course, are now divorced.

The ceremony was held at the county jail, which also functions as the sheriff's office and municipal courthouse, but it seems more jail-like, perhaps because the two floors above are bedecked with razor wire. Letters over the door spell out "Law Enforcement Complex."

A shriveled white guy in a red plaid shirt rolled past in his wheelchair, looked up at us, and divined that we had never been here before. "Y'all need a good lawyer?" he said. "Not yet," Melanie said. The lawyer's client was a querulous cowgirl at the infor-mation/cashier's counter, saying, "Well, I guess I got to. I don't feel like I'm guilty, but I'm gonna just go on and pay it."

Also standing around in the big brick-walled hallway waiting on the Justice of the Peace were a young black couple, the man looking like Scottie Pippen, only shorter, and the woman large and shy, and about ten of their friends and relations. A com-manding woman stood near us, across the chilly hallway from the group, taking photographs. "Crouch down there," she told two women in front, and they gallantly bent their knees to stand trembling until the pictures were taken.

I was carrying a camera, too. After a moment, the boss looked at us, and having exactly assessed the situation, said, "Would y'all like someone to take your picture?" We would; she did.

About this time the judge showed up, a chunky, pleasant man in his thirties, who looked like he fit very snugly in his clothes. He wore glasses. "Everybody come on in here now," the judge said, bustling through a door. "No sense in y'all waitin' in the hall."

It was us, the other much larger wedding party, the cowgirl and her wheelchair-bound lawyer, and a group of three country boys, all with plaid shirts and sullen expressions, son, daddy, and pawpaw, as grandfathers are referred to here in Mississippi. The courtroom felt like a miniature movie theater with seats and a steeply sloping floor. The JP married the black couple first. We all congratulated the bride and Scottie as they walked out. He looked uncertain, but he congratulated me, ahead of time. I felt, as he obviously did, that we were comrades. A woman, one of the judge's assistants, took my camera for more pictures.

Then the judge married us, which took about two minutes. Melanie, in a long black dress, looked wonderful. I wore jeans, a coat and a tie and looked dreadful. When I said, "I do" too early, everyone behind us laughed. I had to allow the judge to finish, and say it a second time.

My new wife was the dearest thing to me, as she had been for twenty years. But we didn't marry for love. Love had always been present, through five houses in four states, jobs, schools, cars, and cats, an extra lover we had for a while, hopes and worries, affairs and arguments, sickness and health, richer and mostly poorer, and so on—the usual record of lives lived together.

Still, we had a reason. While we had always worked, for a long time neither one of us had had conventional jobs. And it had been funny for a while, when someone asked who your health insurer was, to say, "broccoli," but every year it seemed riskier. So only a few years after I got a legitimate and regular job with insurance attached, we decided to do the prudent thing so that we would both be covered. We married, then, for health insurance.

Sure, okay, I thought. I had started loving women when I was about six and the rest of life had been a grueling no-can't-have-her experience, interrupted by some few happy successes and near-successes. Melanie first and foremost, but other women, too, people I wanted to know and some I did. The woman I lived with for ten years before I knew Melanie. The woman with whom I had a turbulent two-year affair in graduate school. A twenty-six-year-old half-Japanese student who looked up at me from a desk after class one day and said something seemed to her "poignant"; for about five years she and I had a non-affair, one of those crippled intimacies which occur when people sadly do the right thing. These were people I loved. Some I still talk to occasionally. In my world I marry them, too.

Marrying anyone felt at least a little like a defeat to me. We had lived our more or less non-standard lives for twenty years, not in the showy way of pop stars or cookie-cutter "rebels," but our own way, nonetheless. For me this habit went back well into childhood. The child looks around at the school and the social commerce of his companions and the professed values of the adults, bewildered, and thinks, "This coat doesn't fit"—a mild discomfort amplified by a deafening self-consciousness. "I do not believe what they seem to believe." Later, insofar as I could manage, I did what I wanted, or sometimes just what I thought was right, and I have paid and paid for it in small, dull ways every day ever since.

It becomes a habit, and an allegiance. Soon, in your understanding of the world, the everywhere-present falsehood, every small, low act by the company you work for or dissembling behavior by the pillars of your society—say, the Usurers National Bank kicks the rate on your credit card to 24.9 percent—attaches itself to the rest of conventional behavior. There's a line directly from the first lie you heard that you knew to be a lie and the manifold lies of the Usurers Bank, and recognizing that, you are confirmed in your disbelief and your own ways of doing things. Eventually, an interesting thing happens—you begin to feel entitled to your odd ways, because you have already paid. If you then break down and do the conventional thing—marry, for instance—it feels like a loss, or a defeat.

This is not a rare or a radical view of experience, I acknowledge. Maybe it's even a commonplace. At its essence, adult life is an increasingly sad series of defeats, as any sentient person knows. It's only a matter of how much it bothers you.

Melanie and I walked out of the jail and found the car where we had parked out front of a bail bondsman's office emblazoned with red and yellow bumper stickers offering his telephone number. Around the corner and down the block we came to a stoplight. I saw Scottie and his bride and their entourage strolling happily along on the sidewalk, and took a photograph out the back windshield of the car. Then the light changed, and we drove on down the street, headed home. "Good luck," I thought, hoping that marriage wouldn't ruin their relationship. Shouldn't; it's just a piece of paper.

A Thirty-Five-Year-Old Book Review

Michael Arlen's *An American Verdict* (Doubleday, 196 pages, $6.95) is, among other things, an index of how seductive paranoia has become. The book is a short history of the aftermath of the December 1969 Chicago "gunbattle" in which Fred Hampton and Mark Clark were killed and four other Black Panthers were wounded. It is also an informal study of the effects of publicity on events. It deals in passing with Chicago history, recent American history and the end of "the revolution." But first of all *An American Verdict* is the story of how the Cook County state's attorney and a handful of policemen shot two black men to death and escaped punishment.

In 1969, Fred Hampton was chairman of the Black Panther Party in Illinois. Arlen describes him this way: ". . . but Fred Hampton had seemed to many to have been a different sort of black activist. He was young. He came from solid people—his father had worked twenty years for Corn Products in nearby Argo. Hampton had played football at Maywood High School, and while there had organized a protest for a community swimming pool. As a Panther, he spoke well, with warmth, and not always with anger."

The police raid occurred two weeks after one Panther and two cops had been killed in a gunfight, and after months of other gunfights, police harassment ("charges dropped"), and close press coverage. Panther headquarters was a shabby two-bedroom apartment on Chicago's West Monroe Street. Nine men and women had been inside when fourteen cops showed up at five in the morning to serve a search warrant for illegal weapons.

Afterward, the public show began. The state's attorney, Edward Hanrahan, issued a series of statements. Hanrahan was important in the political structure and thought to be a likely future mayor; his "Special Prosecutions Unit" had planned and executed the raid. The police who had conducted the raid performed an elaborately rehearsed half-hour reenactment for a local TV station. The statements from Hanrahan and other official sources ran like this:

> As soon as Sergeant Daniel Groth and Officer James Davis, leading our men, announced their office, occupants of the apartment attacked them with shotgun fire. The officers immediately took cover. The occupants continued firing at our policemen from several rooms within the apartment.
>
> Thereafter, three times Sergeant Groth ordered all his men to cease firing and told the occupants to come out with their hands up. Each time, one of the occupants replied, "Shoot it out," and they continued firing at the police officers. Finally, the occupants threw down their guns and were arrested.

Or, at a press conference, behind a table of weapons from Panther headquarters: ". . . I point also to the automatic revolver which was used by Fred Hampton in the course of the attack on the police . . ."

The curious synthesis of Jack Webb and Amy Vanderbilt is more than simple officialese. The man is not only bending the truth, he is also acting (not real well), and acting in a kind of theater in which we have required him to participate. Public reality.

The Chicago police's Internal Investigation Division conducted a quick inquiry into the raid, concluding that the police were blameless. On January 23, 1970, the coroner's jury returned "justifiable homicide." A week later a Cook County grand jury indicted the seven surviving Panthers for attempted murder; the indictments were later withdrawn. A federal grand jury investigated and instead of indictments it produced (May 1970) a "report" which contained FBI findings to the effect that there was physical evidence of one shot by the Panthers and evidence of between eighty-three and ninety-nine shots from the police. Paraffin tests showed that Fred Hampton had not fired a gun. Autopsies disclosed that he had died from two shots through the head and neck, close together, and probably fired at close range. In other words, everything indicated that as Panther Bobby Rush said on the day after the raid, "Hampton was murdered in his sleep."

Still later, in April 1971, a special Cook County grand jury failed to indict the police for the raid itself, but did indict Hanrahan and thirteen others other for "conspiracy to obstruct justice" after the raid. It took four months and the Illinois Supreme Court to get the judge to open the indictment. Eventually Hanrahan and the others were acquitted. In the 1972 elections Hanrahan was voted out of office, apparently by the black wards which delivered for the rest of the Daley ticket.

All of this is presented by Arlen simply, directly, without hysteria. The hysteria is left to us. A lot of these events we all saw in some form in the newspapers and on television. Of course, what we got were the high points spread out over three or four years, and one of the virtues of Arlen's book is assembling it all together. A larger virtue is that his reporting cuts many ways: it's not that gesture which has become so popular—using the instant cant of the left to attack the aged cant of the right. George McGovern comes to town and embraces Daley. Just so no one misses the point, Arlen quotes McGovern: "'The Democratic Party I worked to build in South Dakota is the same Party, and works in the same way, as the Party that Mayor Daley heads here in Illinois.'" Innocuous maybe, but obviously one more actor in the theater of public reality.

And Arlen takes some trouble to characterize the cops. The people and the job. It is reminiscent of a recent newsmagazine story about a liberal Florida criminology professor who joined his local police force and soon found himself taking on many of the attitudes attributed to "pigs." Attitudes in large part shaped by paranoia. Arlen notes that cops had been killed and wounded in the incidents before December 4, 1969. Police seem to deserve much of the responsibility for these incidents, but the dead and wounded friends and fellow cops at least bring clear some motivation. Fear.

And clarity is needed. No one appears very clear-headed in all of this—the cops, the politicians, the press, the public. Even the Panthers, with their bandoleers and berets and boots, are playing in a romantic fantasy (largely pushed on them by whites), and as Arlen says, "in the end we wrapped this fantasy around their necks." The confusion between a simplistic public reality and anything which passes for the-way-things-are is total, and deadly.

No one is very hard on his own ideas. No one seems to wonder very much. The police don't seem to wonder what they might do if they were marked and stuck, more or less permanently, in a slum. The blacks don't seem to wonder whether a couple dozen junior execs from GM, dressed with crossed cartridge belts over their grey flannel suits and carrying M-16's and milling around a lot, might not eventually end up shooting and getting shot by police. The police don't have the time and the Panthers don't have the patience and there is of course no reason why they should.

There's not a lot of what you could call "doubt" on anyone's part. There is a sentence buried in Arlen's book in the description of the cops' "official reenactment" of the raid which says: "It required four hours [to film], members of the CBS crew explained later, partly because some of the policemen used profanity and so sections had to be re-taped . . ."

A stratagem which likely didn't fool anyone. It's difficult to imagine cops shouting, "Gosh!" and "Shucks!" Still, they re-taped. It is the same type of act when George McGovern embraces Daley and the Cook County machine. The purist, who condemns McGovern for it, is just carrying the play one step further. It is clearly not a book for purists.

If the police edit profanity, so do the newspeople who report them. It's not like Dan Rather and Noam Chomsky don't play. A giant public charade encompasses pretty much everything that's important—race, economic advantage, death, sexuality, life as it is actually lived. A simplistic straight-lined "sincerity" is championed, as if people never felt two emotions at the same time. The police re-taped for the same reason Maureen Dean pulled her hair up tight before the Senate Watergate hearings, for the same reason white radicals babble about "the people" when most of the people feel little for them other than hostility, for the same reason McGovern came to Chicago. In service to a wildly oversimplified public reality.

We have public reality because we beg for it. Politicians, the news and entertainment media, the schools, take their existence from it in large part and so have an interest in preserving and extending it. We complain about "bullshit" and ask for plain talk when what we want is oversimplification—bullshit. Plain talk about the raid in Chicago is ultimately too complex and unsatisfactory. Perhaps a facile conception of the culture is necessary to keep us all relatively sane. Perhaps there is no other way to deal at the same time with things happening in the kitchen and New York and Tokyo and Kansas; but teachers and journalists have somehow convinced us that we should. No one feels free not to think something about each personality, event or decision in the parade—stupidity is preferred to ignorance. And general theories are prized because they make sense out of a lot of things easily. I recall an otherwise thoughtful friend casually explaining how "man is naturally aggressive"—I think it explained Vietnam. The teaching and journalism industries are geared to supply theories of this kind; people complain if things don't make sense, if they don't understand. Further, one is pressed to believe the theories. They are "significant" and "meaningful" and provide "understanding." If not, the work of the teacher and the journalist is a little silly. Which, of course, it is.

But the pressure to believe hits a soft spot in the head. Belief makes us feel better. Maybe it is only a natural hatred for the incoherence of our experience and a natural disinclination toward examining our own actions. We want Fred Hampton's murder to make sense, and clearly it never will. Slogans are so much simpler, so much less effort. Glib general theories about our "sick society" and "no real justice" are attractive and give the illusion of an explanation. Details like the FBI's relatively good performance in this case don't fit and have to be ignored because of what we believe. It's not difficult. In matter of fact, though, the culture is huge and diverse, and no sense will be made of it. In matter of fact, "justice" is just something someone made up.

There is really nothing wrong with "public reality" of itself. What is unfortunate is that we have become convinced that we are supposed to believe what we think and what we say. Belief is supposed to order and explain things. But believing tends to lead to coercion. The believer, having solved his own problems, is ready to give the solution to his recalcitrant fellows. To "educate." Maybe he buys himself a gun, or a TV spot. As a form, the opinion is much more humane. You can change an opinion every half hour if you please. No one will die (implicitly, kill) for his opinions.

In this context, Michael Arlen's book is to be valued for what are all the "reactionary" virtues. The pretense toward objectivity. The concentration on detail, small bits of information as opposed to conclusions. And Arlen sees his role as supplying information rather than belief. We, as well as the police and the Panthers, already have too many beliefs, most of which are supported by too little information. This is an imperfectly educated guess, and it is based on two ideas: that the more information one has, the less he believes, and that belief is vicious.

[1973]

IV

A Cubist Take on Teaching

Some Notes on Teaching and Writing

I. What I Did Last Autumn
II. Writing Workshops, a Tiny Testimonial
III. Some TA
IV. First Class (Letter to a Friend)

University teaching may be one of the dullest subjects in the index, but if you spend years doing it, you think about it all the time and you want to talk about it. The best thing I ever read about teaching is in Walker Percy's famous essay, "The Loss of the Creature," and if you haven't read that, you should stop reading this and find it. The image Percy paints of "the great man" as teacher is so lovely that it is about as perfect an imagining, as something to aspire to when you set out to teach, as I can think of. The whole essay is full of wonderful stuff, the kind of writing which might change your life, too good for required reading. My own thoughts are far more mundane, and fragmentary.

In the constant company of people who are younger and less informed than you are, speaking about things you have studied more than they, participating in a transaction with them that you have lived through a hundred times and they've only done once, protected from much in the way of real demands on your abilities or energies by the incompetence and outright cynicism of the worst of your fellow instructors, and working at a task for which you have been hired and toward which much pious lip service is dedicated but to which your superiors are largely indifferent, this is an occupation which threatens one with all manner of poisonous spiritual and psychological diseases, which in familiar terms fall under the general category of being a jerk. None escape.

The following snapshots, each first drafted at a different moment in my teaching experience, each treat a limited corner of a subject with a thousand corners. They are personal notes, nothing more, a sort of cubist sketch of teaching writing in the university.

I wish that I had some more comprehensive and coherent view of teaching, but I don't. As is true of all arts, a comprehensive and coherent view of it is hard to come by and tends to suggest it's smaller than it is. As in other arts, teaching's great seduction is moments when you the artist disappear into the work, forgetting your bloody self. It's part police action, part inspiration; half maieutic practice, half entertainment. I have been—and am—a pretend teacher. After twenty years or so, my most studied notion of what to do amounts to this: Try to open a space in front of them.

I

What I Did Last Autumn

"I won't be in class Friday," the kid said. "I've gotta go squirrel-hunting." My past life as a member of the general public who had attended a number of schools at all levels and spent in aggregate about twenty years in the educational system, and so felt himself to know a thing or two about education and ready to weigh in with an opinion, had not really prepared me to reply. I was nonplussed. I nodded.

I was handing out teacher evaluation sheets, that perfect flowing together of sixties' idealism and the consumer culture, which suggests the student consider his or her education as an extension of breakfast, their teacher another bowl of cereal. Pretty much the way the general public already thinks of it.

"Stimulates interest in the subject matter?" the evaluation sheet asks. "Keeps students' attention? Overall quality of the course as a learning experience? Use a No. 2 pencil; mark A, B, C, D, or F." By and large the students are very kind to the cereal.

Last August, after years of wandering in the wilderness, I was hired on as a college instructor in grammar and composition at a rate comfortably above the minimum wage but a little shy of what a good BMW mechanic might earn. I was ecstatic to get the job; a hundred other people wanted it.

I had taught a class or two as a graduate assistant on my way to an advanced degree, but like everyone else who instructs at the college level, I had started in the classroom with almost no training as a teacher. Understand, I'm not sure that's a bad thing. Not at all.

Last week a girl asked me about "that animal" I had talked about on Thursday. The Sphinx. She's a bright girl, talks a lot, charming in her way.

The students are pretty much all charming. The ones who have never heard of the Sphinx. The ones who turn in essays copied from travel brochures and old textbooks. The ones who write "they was" and "he were." The ones who sleep sitting up. And finally and especially, the ones who are curious, although by the time they reach college there are too few of those.

Some students want to learn. For others, though, words like "work" and "learn" are old-fashioned expressions, and if your teacher uses them, drop the course. "Learning," to many of them, is an essentially passive process similar to sitting in the driver's seat while a chain drags your car through a dark corridor of soap, water, and huge rolling blue brushes. Just as an automatic carwash produces half-clean cars, schools tend to produce half-educated students.

When I came from Johns Hopkins to a large state university in Louisiana, one of my new colleagues said, "You know, the students here aren't going to be like your students at Hopkins." After four months here, I think, "How are they different?" The Hopkins kids were brighter, that's true, but the similarities overwhelm the difference.

In both places, the basic relationship between teacher and student is the same. Besides age and an addiction to MTV, students everywhere share one other defining experience. They have been in school for the past twelve years. They know about school. If the first thing you learn up at the front of the room is that students are charming and loveable, the second thing you learn is that teachers are not, at least not necessarily.

The teacher is the authority, the cop, the person who is forcing the student to be present somewhere he does not want to be and to do work he does not want to do. In a more sinister way, from the university administration's point of view, the police function extends to weeding out those who aren't equipped for college, who aren't going to be here four years, or two. It had never occurred to me that this was a tacit part of my task, that freshman classes were a clumsy extension of the admissions process, or a corrective to it.

The teacher is also seen, by the public and, oddly, by the university as well, as the carrier of "knowledge" which he or she is charged with supplying to the students. This transaction is imagined either as a transfer of goods, like so much grain or gasoline, or as detail work, in which the teacher is seen as the person to polish up the student with knowledge, more or less the way the three guys at the end of the dark corridor polish up the car with wax. This is "stimulating interest" and providing a "learning experience."

Unsuspecting, you walk into a cinderblock walled room where twelve people are thinking about dancing or squirrel-hunting, and twelve others are looking at you expectantly, waiting for their souls to be saved. An oversimplification, of course; most of them have both of these attitudes plus other subsidiary ones. Okay, let's see, how to begin? You could maybe start with, "The coordinating conjunction joins grammatical elements of equal rank . . ." No, that ain't going to get it. That's school.

Well before he arrives at college every student has been taught that work is something to be avoided, that learning is work, and that if it's boring, it's learning. The curiosity he was born with has been largely educated out of him. The teacher is up against various problems but one of the toughest is the student's past experience of school. Taking up the roll book and chalk, I underestimated the task.

I was in a situation which I had not been trained for and for which the training would likely be pathetically inadequate, if it were anything like most of the other "ideas" and rules which make up the whole fabric of the university's self-image. So, as I suspect most new teachers do, I did the only reasonable thing—I panicked. Out of this panic one draws the energy and the imagination to teach oneself to teach.

The first thing to do, I soon figured out, was to forget everything you thought you knew about education when you were a member of the general public. The second thing was to strike a new attitude toward the forms of education—policies, tests, rules, grades, and so on—which universities love and faculty revolutionaries hate, each centering their thinking on themselves instead of on their task. A good attitude was somewhere between fondness and indifference. Much classroom time is spent having a class and pretending to learn things; wouldn't it be possible to reverse that, to play at having a class and actually learn things? And finally I thought maybe I could go back to the rudiments of the project, and reduce teaching to basics or essence. For much of the time I spent in school, I did exactly what my students now do. Faced with this new problem—how to teach—I have tried to remember how I learned.

A few years ago I bought an old automobile and, because I had no money and loved mechanical things anyway, learned to repair cars. I read books and went to parts joints, junk yards, and the shop of a very elegant, very painstaking, and endlessly tolerant mechanic. He seemed to take a kind of joy in the work. He showed me things—what to watch out for, how a torque wrench works, what an "interference fit" was. Remembering him, I made a photocopy of a photograph of the Sphinx from an encyclopedia, and delivered it.

From school, I best remember one of my undergraduate history professors. He loved his subject, not in a "Gosh, isn't it wonderful?" sort of way—he would carve it up, explain it, tease it, make fun of it, complain—but he was clearly hooked. He was himself an illustration in how it was possible to care. He liked details, and he liked imagination. Each class period he quickly got lost in his subject. He did not pretend to be more interested in our education than we were.

Thinking about them, I notice patterns. What it comes down to is not simply that people teach themselves, although that's an essential idea. It is that learning—and learning almost anything—is one of the great pleasures of being alive. That by the time I get my students they not only do not know this, they have been actively persuaded otherwise—actively taught otherwise, if you will. That we should be teaching people to wonder as much as to know, and that we don't.

I am learning to teach; it is hard work, but finally, a pleasure. The principal function of a teacher seems to be to say, "Hey, look at this. Hey, take this wrench, poem, verb—look what it is, look what it does, look what you can do with it. Hey, look." The students look at their fingernails, out the window, or up into the trees, for squirrels. So I'm still learning.

II

Writing Workshops, a Tiny Testimonial

I have done construction work, driven delivery trucks and taxi-cabs, sold door to door, repaired cars, washed dishes, clerked in a store, run guns to Ethiopia. I did these things, as well as writing advertising, PR, speeches, poems, plays, reviews, journalism, and fiction, for seventeen years before attending the Writing Seminars at Johns Hopkins. Still, I get letters from noted editors saying that the writing in the stories I have sent is "characteristic of so many people who spend their time in writing programs." No doubt the eight and a half months I spent in Baltimore made my prose "workshoppy."

At Hopkins my writer friends had similarly sloppy backgrounds. One, at nineteen, had flown to Paris on earnings from waitressing in a rot-gut steakhouse, landing at Orly knowing not a soul; by the time she got to graduate school she was thirty-two. One had been a social worker, among other things. Another, a lawyer. Yet another had spent some years wandering from Chicago to the southwest, there working day labor and sleeping in fleabag hotels and jails in New Mexico, Texas, and Louisiana.

So it was odd to read of another commentator, who as an editor helped bring Portnoy to a wider public, saying, "We should stop wasting programs on the young," and advocating a minimum age of twenty-five "so they have something to write about besides growing up, family, going to school, and falling in love." Always safest to suggest things that have already been done, I guess, but I wonder. If love and family are no longer worthy subjects (please, not a word to Tolstoy), what should one write about? Self-abuse? What a famous guy one is?

If the choice is between getting advice such as the above, and getting it from John Barth and Stephen Dobyns and whoever's at Iowa, I'll take the latter. If the writers now talk in classrooms instead of cafes, that's sad, but it's tough all over. Our literary criticism once came from Coleridge; today, Carolina.

It's not necessary, is it, to say much about the dull but immensely popular remarks imagining a dread uniformity and timidity of prose written in workshops? This idea, a favorite of both really dim-witted critics and really bad writers who think themselves "radical," is nonsense worthy of a spot in Flaubert's famous *Dictionary*.

HAT HAT HAT. Who cannot be "strange" and "experimental" at a click of the keys?

Some of the writing in workshops is imitative, some is facile, some is garbage. So what? How does this differ from the backlist of any publisher, the contents of any great old big or little magazine, even the collected works of any great writer? Some is genius. You go to the workshop and there you have (another) year trying to find that in yourself. You have friends to help. They have IQs big enough to knock a house down. They have cheap clothes, nice hair. They make fun of you. They read books. They argue. Do they write like you? Nah. The people I knew at Hopkins had their faults, God knows, but there wasn't a sheep in the bunch.

Meanwhile you've got a place to hang around, doing something that you feel is worth doing, and doing it in the midst of other people who feel the same way. You see the work through other people's eyes. In "fixing" their sentences, you learn something about your own. "Rewriting" their stories, you learn something about stories in general.

If you're lucky, the conversation in the writing program is in the writer's language, which is neither the language of English composition ("coordinate and subordinate levels of generality within the paragraph") nor the language of contemporary literary criticism (here insert your favorite atrocity). The writer's language, based in metaphor, is the maker's language, as opposed to the analyst's or critic's. Critics often speak in metaphors, too, I guess, but most are so dreadfully bad at it.

Say you try to make a beagle. You need to think about the tail, and not first about the insidious socioeconomic code it "inscribes." First, you have to attach the damn thing; to live, the dog must wag. Look here (one of your sadly underexperienced classmates says), Each time your dog wags this tail, it falls off. Maybe try it a little more . . . vague. Flexible. Vague it up. "Vague-up?" A verb likely not in the critic's vocabulary (nor anyone else's).

This new notion of holy vagueness makes of vagueness something which you maybe hadn't thought of before, a thing more complicated and richer than the old vagueness, which we all know, is wholly bad. Useful to a writer, not to a critic. The critic judges and deconstructs in language which is as deliciously subtle as it is toplofty. Still, try to make a beagle using the critic's syntax, and your dog's a manx.

You go for the muckety-muck, the star, and you find the people. They think writing is important, not because it cures anomie or sells popcorn or pads the vita, not for any clear-cut reason. They have this silly and thunderous faith. So do you. The muckety-muck contributes. The school leaves you alone, by and large, maybe even gives you money. I'm too old to go to law school, you think. Thank God.

Someone's talking about your story. She's wrong, of course; she's an idiot, an imbecile, a total loss. You don't care about her damn GRE scores, she might as well be carpet. She's wrong for this and this and this and this reason, and not only that—

But at this point, something occurs to you. Twist this sentence she's abusing, just a notch, and . . .

Later, of course, you want her back. She was so tall. In the hall that day, she said, "I don't know, Steve, I think I could take ya." She made the work better. She, and the workshop.

III

Some TA

A few years ago, when my sister was looking for colleges for her genius sons, she told me that she wouldn't send one to such and such a school, because "all he would see for the first two years would be teaching assistants." I nodded and thought, What an ignorant thing to say. This wasn't my sister's idea, I realized, but a notion from what she'd been reading, college guides and handbooks, whose estimate of the sorry abilities of graduate teaching assistants is received wisdom. You can find the same automatic contempt for university teaching assistants in magazines and newspapers, in the opinions of university professors or administrators, or on earnest television "special reports" about higher education. A student I had last semester identified her instructor in the previous course in the sequence as "some TA." I still think, What an ignorant thing to say.

Teaching assistants are in fact some of the best teachers in any English department, and I suspect in all other departments. Not all teaching assistants, of course. Like the regular faculty, some TAs are excellent and some are awful and most are in between. But if you work in the university, you find the most disheartening thing about it is not the students' happy ignorance or the TA's cheerful inexperience or the college administration's merry bungling, but some colleagues' grim indifference to their work.

As an undergraduate, I learned more from a TA than from any other teacher, and I never even had a class with him. He was a linguist and writer, interested in what I was interested in. Eventually he would become a famous art critic, win a MacArthur grant. Now, twenty-five years later, I recall a line he once wrote, admonishing himself: "I realize, as well, that writing criticisms of the university ranks second only to the Frisbee as the principal occupation of third-rate minds." Now, though, he's admonishing me.

As a teaching assistant, I initially felt like a hero because I was supplementing out of my own pocket the meager photocopy allowance the department provided. I felt heroic until I realized that all my friends were doing it too. They were being paid four or five hundred dollars a month and spending some of it to copy this poem or that essay to give to their students. They were staying up all night marking papers. They were spending hours outside of class time "conferencing" with students. When not sitting around together somewhere having passionate conversations about literature, they were sitting around together having passionate conversations about—teaching.

At first these habits carry over when a TA gets a job and becomes a regular faculty member. The two years I was a lecturer, teaching five courses a term, the lecturers did the same things TAs had. I noticed, though, that such interest in teaching was less common in the upper ranks of the professoriat. The game in the regular faculty is not spending your own money on teaching; it's getting to the departmental travel budget early in the semester before your fellow professors can rifle the cashbox. For many, passionate conversations are gone, too, unless you can call an intense desire to sound smart a passion. And it is not about teaching assistants that students have come to me and said, nervous and bewildered, "You know, it's like she hates literature."

Teaching assistants are often young and inexperienced. But most of them are not venal or cynical or worn out. Teaching for many of them is a transforming experience. At my school, I informally supervise the teaching assistant chosen to teach the introductory short story writing course. Not long ago this assignment, which is envied, was given to a graduate student with a crippling and tiresome inability to be serious about anything. He was so busy conning you with sham earnestness that he apparently had no idea how transparent the sham was. He wrote well, but his work was cool—his heart wasn't in it. I worried about the job he would do in teaching the introductory course. I needn't have. He turned into Mary Poppins.

The guy was all over me, all semester long, wanting to know about this, wanting advice about that, wanting to show me a story some student had written, asking if I had a handout about this, how to get this other thing across, wanting to tell me how "good!" these sophomores are, how some of them were the equal of his classmates in graduate workshops. I said, "Yeah, I know the feeling." He was different now, willing to care about something and to show it. After the semester ended, he became just one of several TA's asking about pet students' luck in the subsequent short story writing course which I teach.

I am not arguing that TA's are always better teachers than the so-called "stars" of higher education. I am only arguing that the situation is far more complex and mysterious than comparing a teaching assistant to a star and assuming you'll get better instruction from the latter. Most departments only have two or three stars anyway, so the real comparison is between teaching assistants and middle management types.

In my experience some stars are little more than glorified clerks, puffed up folks to avoid. But other stars are legitimately called that, and the caring and intelligence and hard work that have enabled them to write and publish more than their less intense colleagues goes into their teaching as well as into their research. All that these people know is intelligence and drive and they apply it to whatever they're involved in. They have done that their whole lives. They have been brilliant a long time. Once, of course, they were teaching assistants.

IV

First Class (Letter to a Friend)

Some emergency notes to ease you into the project—

1) The main and major thing no one ever tells you about is the stage fright. It is quite literally sickening. It tends to last, in severe form, only for the first two or three weeks of every semester. After twenty-five or so courses, I feel it in only slightly diminished form every September and January. Maybe it's worse for the poisonously self-conscious and maybe it gets better later on, but everyone I've ever talked to has acknowledged it when asked, while almost never does anyone bring it up. The students are afraid, too, they say, and I think that's true, as much (or more) of each other as of you. The thing they're most afraid of is having to talk in front of each other. And Laurence Olivier used to puke before plays (this last I found very reassuring). The one thing I do after some experience in this business is just to say whatever comes into my head, a way maybe of keeping the distance between the public self and the private self down to a mildly painful minimum—too much stretching of that distance hurts too much. So I discuss my clothes in a simple but beguiling way ("pretty nice coat, don't y'all think? I graduated from high school in this coat") or some TV show or how fond I am of aspirin and the Bayer company for providing them, crossed with those

little letters, how dependable they have been, or the new Wal-Mart and how much it has improved life here in Hattiesburg. I then and thus likely fall into the category of "off-the-wall," which is okay, just one of the categories that the students have ready for their teachers. I also mumble a lot, so I fall into that category, too. Past this sort of categorization, they don't think about teachers very much ("scatterbrain" is an awful lot of thought work for a 101 student, so don't worry about that).

2) The performance. It is a performance, a show. Make no mistake about it. It's also a mess. A seamless performance it ain't. (And sometimes, largely with luck, it's also a conversation. Sometimes they find they like to talk and do. But that happens later, and one finds one's own ways of encouraging it. Note that I say "encouraging" not "creating.") But it's a mess. I often bump into things on purpose, as well as a great many theatrical pauses, dumb jokes ("Now say the ship just went down and so you're out there, in the middle of the Atlantic Ocean, in the rubber raft, and each one of those words weighs, say, ten pounds . . . you gonna keep that whole paragraph? Every word? How about this 'I think I want to discuss' stuff . . ." etc).

3) Persuade yourself that more than half the responsibility is theirs. It is, and one persuades oneself eventually anyway. But sooner is better than later. In any case, you will always work more and harder than they do. Sometimes one will remind you, yeah, but you're getting paid. To which the correct reply is "handsomely" and a smile.

4) In the first class of the first course I taught, at Hopkins, I had a black girl say, "I hate readin', and I hate writin'." Her name was Rayvelle. Like in any good TV movie, she later thought the class was wonderful. She may have even learned something. And she wrote pretty well (not a result of anything I did; she came in writing pretty well; go figure). Later in

Louisiana, at Monroe, in one class when I was going through the introductory first day stuff ("What's your name, where you from, how you think the Saints are going to do this year? Looks like snow to me, you think it's gonna snow?" etc), from the back of the room some kid says, "You look nervous. Why don't you sit down?" Long pause. Then I looked back at him and said, "That's good. The stuff about 'nervous.' Keep that in." At other times, nothing came to me. So, shrug. In all but a few cases, the students are kindly disposed toward their teachers. It's school they don't like, and even those feelings are mixed. A lot of the work in teaching is undoing damage done, sometimes inadvertently, sometimes not, by previous teachers.

I recommend Walker Percy's essay "The Loss of the Creature" which is in his book *The Message in the Bottle.*

5) Dismissing the class early is always a good plan, one I use frequently. I also sometimes take a careful and extended look out the window, and say, "Looks like it's going to be windy next Thursday . . . Paul, what do you think? Think Thursday's gonna be windy?" Paul says some powerful wind going to blow up long about Thursday (Paul has been pre-selected for this duty, he's a wiseass). "Can't have English class in all that wind, I don't think." And then, because some are always slow: "No class on Thursday."

6) I have more than once labored over some student all semester long and then taught him or her in a fifteen minute conversation in the hall after the last class meeting that which I had failed to teach him or her in fifteen weeks and forty-five hours of classes during the semester. The point: anybody who thinks he can predict how this all works is foolish.

7) You can't simultaneously teach twenty-four people bowling. Why they think you can teach writing this way is still a mystery to me.

8) The textbooks are rated in degrees of awful. Most are written not for the students, but to protect the authors from their colleagues. The one we had last year talked about "coordinate and subordinate levels of generality within the paragraph." This of course was hugely beneficial to a bunch of eighteen-year-olds trying to get through school and some of whom who may have had some interest, maybe mild, in learning writing.

Textbooks which do try to speak directly to the students tend to be icky in the extreme, like any oldster trying to speak "young." Groovy, baby. Beware the temptation to try to connect with the students in this way. Beware the temptation to pretend you are not the adult, the authority. You will not fool them. You are the authority, much as we all hate it. When I went to Texas as an undergraduate, there was a professor who actually wore a Nehru jacket around campus, a figure of some fun. On the other hand, today, fifteen years later, he's a dean. Depends what your dreams are made of, I guess.

I make fun of the textbooks on a regular basis (some students hate it, it undermines their sense that God's in His heaven, etc.—but somebody's got to tell them) and when I have my wits about me, tell the students, "You're not wrong. You're not crazy. This is fake-o technological language which barely makes any sense. But the last half of the chapter gets sort of interesting. But this part—this is, in fact, bad writing."

8A) Footnote. The students do like structure, some overall picture; no matter how simple. Thus the syllabus (which, I was told, everyone forgets about after the first two weeks, and this has turned out to be true, or only a slight exaggeration, at least in my classes)—the syllabus makes students feel less adrift. You don't have to follow it.

Structure, a sense of control or something, is also why you tell them what you're going to do and then do something resembling what you said you were going to do (I often forget).

It is also well to try to tie this week's class to last week's (done by making plenty of references to the past or next class whether apt or not—ex: "Last week we said a lot of stuff about sentences, today I want to talk about paragraphs—a place for them ole sentences to go").

9) Tell them what you think, the best stuff, as clearly as you can. Sometimes—often, really, you have to simplify it. Always you have to illustrate it. And you have to say everything at least twice.

There's a lot of native intelligence which shows up in the students and not just in the ones you expect it from; they respond to you sometimes just because you say something that makes human sense. You have this sticky role as intermediary between them and the authorities and they've already heard the bullshit rationales and the high rhetoric which the authorities don't live up to themselves. So you have to figure out things you haven't thought about in years, or ever.

Ex: "Why learn to write in a language nobody talks in?"

"Well, the fancy answer is that words are precise tools designed for precise uses, and while you could use a crescent wrench as a hammer, whatever work you're doing will go smoother, it'll be more elegant, if you hammer with a hammer, wrench with a wrench. You want your brain surgeon saying, 'Hey, dude, flip me the thingamabob'? The less fancy answer is that some people do talk in this language and they have all the money and power, it's like a club. It's like wearing a clean shirt; other people, especially those in the club, are going to be more likely to hear you out, take you seriously, hire you, let you in the club, if you're wearing a clean shirt."

Ex 2: "Why are all these writers writing about sex?"

"Well, Larry, think a minute. What's interesting?"

10) Use the blackboard. Corny, but it works. Sometimes, when you turn your back, giggling breaks out. It's not often about you—they aren't that interested. It mostly reflects their feel-

ing of being out from under the thumb of authority for a glorious few seconds. The blackboard is the most powerful visual aid you've got. It'll make you feel like a schoolmarm. That's all right. You are a schoolmarm, in much the same way you are the authority. Your voice and the blackboard. And Xerox Corp.

11) Expect to forget things, assign the same thing twice, misspeak, spend all night grading papers and then forget to bring them to class, etc.

12) The quality of attention, when one is talking to twenty-five people at the same time, is very low, and this has to be figured into the mix. However obvious it is, it took me a while to comprehend this. The sharpest illustration is that moment when some kid raises his or her hand and asks the question which you have just spent five minutes answering.

13) Remember that you are teaching the ones that are not like you at all as well as the ones who are made in your image. The tendency, or temptation, is to favor those students who remind you of you at that age, and it's almost unavoidable, so maybe the best thing to do is simply to recognize it and try to do it less. A corollary tendency is to teach the way you wish you had been taught. That's fine, but try to remember that it's a less swell fit for people who are some other way. This is also one of the problems of teaching twenty-five at a time.

14) They rise to your expectations.

15) Students are also the biggest bunch of weasels in the world. This came as a surprise to me, so I pass it along.

16) Your colleagues are the most disappointing and disheartening thing about teaching. The students are okay.

17) It is, finally, a rich experience. Sometimes it works and that is wonderful. We assume it works a great deal more than we see, because we have a good attitude. But when you see it, it's wonderful. It is also something worth doing, in the large sense, which cannot easily be said of a lot of other work. It is also, as you say, fun, sometimes. When you have a good day, or a good class, it's great. But there's no way to ensure that. You try to increase the odds, is all.

18) Be a little careful. In some weird way, you have a lot of power, even though it feels like you don't have any.

19) Let's review. Stage fright is normal, and diminishes considerably three weeks into the semester. Tolerate the messiness. They like you, to the extent they care. They're scared, mostly of each other.

It's really a coaching job. Consider the implications.

I forgot. Many of the people who teach writing know nothing about it, like zip. So you're way ahead there. Many are not super bright. Advantage, you. Some—and this in my callow way I found stunning—don't even care. Or maybe it's care enough. Game, set, and match. Sometimes when I feel bad because I feel like I'm doing a sorry job, I look around, and think, If I wasn't doing it, somebody worse would. A rationalization I recommend.

21) A good teacher knows how little he or she will accomplish and nonetheless tries to shake the world. Teach us to care and not to care, the poet said, Teach us to sit still. That's beautiful.

22) As my dear sister advised me a long time ago in some equally difficult context: One bumbles one's way through.

Bumble, bumble, bumble.

V

Thousand-Word Wisecracks

Enough Already

I tried to think of a personal rule I use in making stories and came up with nothing, such things usually being so much second nature as to be, if not unconscious, at least forgotten. It's the same problem that sometimes occurs in teaching undergraduates when you throttle some poor child for switching point of view in the middle of a sentence, say, and then have to remember—because you have to say—why not. Or worse, on those slow days when you start wondering if any of the things you teach could be shown to be present in your own work and, of course, can't think of any. Then I tried to think whether I ever had had a rule, and then recalled one, though one which had nothing to do with images or significant detail or Aristotelian dramatic structure. It was: no more cats.

It wasn't always so. When I started out cats were in every story and in most of the non-fiction pieces as well, in spite of that other rule that says that when the conversation turns to cats, it's time for the host to start cleaning up and the guests to go home. Still, you write about things you're passionate about, if you have any sense at all, and cats were such for me, one in particular, a gray fellow who was one of my tutors way back when.

For example, I wrote of a separating couple quarrelling over who gets the cat, stealing it back and forth, or in another piece a picture of the sleepy cat on the bedspread watching the telephone beside him ring; it's the boyfriend, long distance for the girlfriend, imagining the cat, longing for its serenity. There's a story about a talking cat, of course, another made of wood, one with a limp wrist and gold eyes who begs like a dog, and one that walks upright—everybody calls him "Tutu." By the time I published a collection, the few reviewers all mentioned this predilection, perhaps alerted by John Barth, another of my tutors, who had kindly consented to write a jacket blurb, in which he noted the crowd of cats inside.

At which point I swore off fictional cats. Could've switched to dogs, which I also like, but that seemed like cheating, like writing those stories which are certainly not about a writer** (as the catechism requires them not to be) but instead feature a beguiling but troubled painter, jeweler, architect, musician, ad man, or ne'er-do-well who in his/her off hours talks very fancy and broods about Laszlo Moholy-Nagy and such. More cleverly, it's an intellectually tilted plumber. Dogs were a dodge.

So I had a rule: No stories in which a cat played any significant part (cousin of another rule, enforced on students, concerning Elvis). And I did it, succeeded. I wrote at least a half a dozen pieces, maybe eight, maybe ten. A prominent snake, a coachwhip, figured in one, and a number of others concerned children, which I think of as sort of cat surrogates, but not a real cat in sight.

And these stories weren't all that bad, by which I mean they weren't any worse than the feline-equipped stories which preceded them. If you could tell that there was a hole in the story, a yawning—strike that—a gaping space where the cat was absent, I didn't notice, couldn't tell. In the whole (unpublished) second collection, there were probably no more than two or six cats. I was cured.

Still, one needs an obsession, damned hard to write without one. I wrote about cars and lawns. There were a number of pieces featuring old people. I've always been sort of interested in the Catholic Church, in which I was raised in the last of its real hoodoo days; I could use that. But I wouldn't say it's an obsession, exactly.

And, anyway, if artists can paint the same painting over and over, Ad Reinhardt with all his black squares and such, or Monet producing haystack after haystack, and if Fitzgerald can write his rich girls again and again, if Chekhov's Vanyas and Jean Rhys' Mr. Mackenzies can reappear with their names changed in play after play and novel after novel . . . what's the big deal? Gee, James, can't you write about something besides focking Ireland!? Sure, I'm not them, I know; it's not the same thing, I know. Cats, Jesus. So I've got third-rate obsessions. What can I say? It's God's will.

My new rule is that lines in a rag-right typescript must come out roughly the same, within two or three or four characters of each other; this I find returns writing to what it always should be—a form of play—although it also sometimes requires the insertion of useless words (which is how "or four" got into this sentence), or the deletion of *le mot juste. C'est la vie.*

Rules are essential. Make yourself some, all you want, strong, logical, bracing, inviolable, iron rules. Feel shame when you break them, and delicious moral superiority when you don't. Nothing is more entertaining. After I wrote the ten cat-less stories, a predictable thing happened. Cats snuck in. Sidled in. In the latest story, nineteen of them. And I've started work on a novel. Stars a veterinarian.

Forget Mercurochrome

Of course, children have no tails, but I don't hold that against them. A child is small and cute and soft. But suppose that you didn't have to wash it or send it to college and you never had to wonder how you had "let it down," where you had "gone wrong with it," or how much its bail was likely to be. Suppose, in other words, that you have a cat instead. Suppose with your savings in pre- and post-natal medical charges, you go to, say, the Virgin Islands for six weeks. A cat offers all the benefits of owning a child, and you can neuter it before it starts playing Metallica CDs. And everyone applauds this politically correct surgery. With time, the cat's advantages only grow. For instance . . .

You can't give a child a silly name. Call a child "Pom-Pom" or "Standard Oil" and the child is sure to come under withering fire later on, in school, from his or her fellows who nowadays are all named more respectable things like Caitlin and Jimi. The child will run home weeping and blame you and rename itself Klik or Z'gllxe, and then coerce you into using this new replacement name of its own devise. A cat, on the other hand, always accepts whatever ludicrous thing you want to call it. Anything you're willing to call out into the neighborhood darkness, it's willing to come to. Eventually.

Buy a cat a watch? Whoever heard of such a thing? A child, on the other hand, will be caterwauling for a timepiece before you've finished paying the hospital. This would be the very same child that is never on time, anyway, who somehow makes you feel guilty for buying it the watch, by interpreting the watch, the one it asked for, as a reproach for its own tardiness, and who loses the watch a week or two weeks, or if you're fortunate, three weeks later on. By now perhaps you have astutely deduced the resemblance between the watch and dozens or perhaps hundreds of other things that a child demands but to a cat are a matter of indifference. So let the watch stand for all those strollers, cribs, car seats, wedding Barbies, Duplos, Legos, CozyCoupes, Nintendoes, Walkpersons, horses, cell phones, iPods and Jaguars which bore the average cat.

You may, though, have overlooked the fact that the cat is (often, usually) covered in fur, which constitutes its clothes, so to speak, a single, infinitely durable, self-expanding, self-replacing outfit that the cat is content, even pleased, to wear, every day, for its entire life. So, choose a cat and you can forget Reeboks, Asics, Adidas, Nikes, and platform shoes, cowboy boots, T-shirts, Gap Kids, Talbots for kids, Ralph Lauren for kids, shirts with holes, jeans with holes, double-dyed, stonewashed, acid-washed, wishwashed blue and all other color jeans, in all sizes. If you like, maybe out of sheer gratitude at the malling that you have been spared, you might buy your cat a sweater.

One often has children when one is young and still believes in love, money, success, real estate, and odd-looking Audis. That is, one makes this dreadful misstep before one has learned that life's supreme aspiration and sweetest pleasure is peace and quiet. Children wiggle, worse than poodles. They have a penchant for screaming. The cat, politely, screams outside, if it screams at all, walks like a whisper, watches no television, and never slams a door. The cat learns far more quickly than any child how little is worth saying.

None of this speaks to what is perhaps the cat's greatest virtue. While for a child you might be required to set an example of impossibly saintly behavior, the cat knows how to forgive. So if you are prone to failure and low behavior, the cat is easily the better choice. If your day customarily is rich in laziness, mendacity, error, foolishness, sycophancy, venality, clumsiness, and (inadvertent, inadvertent) drooling, still you can, in the evening, look into your cat's eyes and see only love. At least indifference. Maybe a little hunger.

Things which might be indelibly imprinted on the child's impressionable little consciousness, the cat takes a more mature view of. Use a dated expression—say, "far out" or "the cat's pajamas," and the cat, Sphinx-like, is unconcerned. Put on an Animals record, and the cat barely blinks. Make some slimy, invidious remark about a coworker, the cat forgives. Take out your frustration over some personal failure in some childish manner—say, screaming at the cat—and the cat, under the couch with only a slight air of superiority, eventually forgets. What a generous beast.

About the most depressing thing about children is their atrocious taste and execrable judgment. A cat, by comparison, will never admire a Robert Altman movie or Madonna's "talent" or chose Wendy's if it can have a bacon double cheeseburger. A cat is not likely to wreck the car or shoplift or hang around in filthy apartments with half a dozen emaciated chums taking drugs. Better yet, the cat won't even do things that lead you to wonder whether it's doing these things. True, if you fail to neuter it early, the cat will get some other cat pregnant—but if so, all that results is more cats, not more children. If you do have it neutered, the cat accepts this setback, I must say, with amazingly good grace.

While we love children, we hate them, as well, and the reason is that they're young, younger than us, and will always be so. Not a cat. One of the most blessed aspects of the cat is that he gets older more quickly than you do, so while you still manage to stumble about with a certain verve, he's taking a nap, one of his many naps. After about two years, the cat is an adult. Five, he's middle-aged, after which begins a very long and contented old age. One of my own cats has been a "senior" for about eight years now. He's right over there, sleeping.

The wife, of course, never fully shared my advanced views concerning cats and children. She's happier now, I'm sure, wherever she is.

A cat is not only small, cute, and soft. In contrast to the child, which spends its entire life trying to leave you, the older a cat gets, the more he hangs around, stays home, keeps you company. He is generous, forgiving and economical, and as indifferent to your flaws of character and foolish old view of life as he is to your foreign policy. He's quiet. He sits on windowsills. He blinks seductively. All that, plus a tail.

Beautiful Deuces

Austin, TX—A tiny little-known unheralded and underfinanced research facility in Austin has published some astonishing findings that promise an imminent and permanent return to good times. With only rudimentary equipment ("For $1.49, it's a pretty good lighter") and a staff of two, S. T. B. Laboratories has just completed a ten-year study of money.

Working for many years with conventional bills—ones, fives, tens, twenties—the S. T. B. team made little progress. When field experiments with foreign currencies ("We spent gourds and gourds in Haiti") turned out to be a dead end, the scientists briefly considered abandoning the project. But the team persevered, and last January things started shaking. A preliminary report to be issued this week advances a startling discovery supported by incontrovertible proof: simply put, S. T. B. has discovered that the two-dollar bill can buy happiness.

Reacting with uncharacteristic dispatch, the federal government is planning a mass distribution of the bills by Christmas. Each citizen is to get one bill. But resistance to the giveaway is already coming from a remarkable range of opponents.

"It sounds good," says one ranking Republican lawmaker. "And we're four-square against anything that sounds good." The president, with the people's good at heart, is carefully avoiding discussion of the matter so as not to offend party members in anticipation of running in 1976.

Democrats are even less enthusiastic. "Misery," says one senior party worker, "is our bread and butter. We get about ninety-eight percent of the misery vote. Of course there are a great many more miserable people than rich people so we always win. Now what's going to happen on election day when those millions of miserable souls stay home, giggling?"

A Harvard economist also counsels caution: "Well, now, you see, frankly, the spiral historically has been consistent, you see, whether it's been stagflating, resuscitating, addlepating, crunching, or whatever, the spiral has always been right side up. Now you go and turn the spiral upside down with a harebrained idea like this and what do you get? You get a goddamn tornado, that's what you get!"

"It'll wreck the economy," predicts a corporate hero. "Not to mention, incidentally, our firm. I mean, right now it's easy to persuade people that they need these goods, and the reason is that they're not happy. That's how we do it. We trick 'em. Then there's labor to consider. With these happy two's around, how am I going to get anybody to sweep or type or load trucks or call me 'sir' for one-fiftieth of what I make? This funny money—are we going to keep our heads about it? Will I get fifty times as much?"

Journalists also voice reservations. "We watch the trend," says one. "Like when the trend was hard-driving, gin-guzzling, idiosyncratic, maverick iconoclasts in sneakers, we went out and bought sneakers. With all this happiness going around, the trend is going to be 'good news,' you know, 'Boy's Pet Turtle Returns, Absent Two Years, Rich Experiences on the Road'—that sort of thing. Sissy stuff."

An authors' alliance comments, "It's not real happiness." And sugar therapies are angrily preparing to cope with huge unsold inventories of awareness, consciousness, and psychic Geiger counters.

Nonetheless, in Washington authorities have ordered a rush printing of 225 million of the beautiful deuces, disguising the action as a bicentennial doggle. Sensing the hostility of vested interests and with the people's good at heart, the president has roughed out a political end run which is not entirely legal but not entirely not. Much in the manner of Meriwether Lewis, the chief executive plans to hand-deliver the magic bills in late December. He has rented a white beard and a red suit. He is coming, America. Hold on.

Random Telephone

The telephone sits on the table like a small black dog. Perhaps you have a green, red, yellow, or white individual. Do not stare at the telephone because pretty soon it will look to you like a small dog, and one that is about to jump—on or at you. In this respect the telephone is like a poodle, dachshund, or other small dog that jumps around, wiggles, yaps, and slobbers, generally making a person very uncomfortable unless the person is the dog's owner. There is something in the master-dog relationship which enables the master figure to endure and even overlook an incredible amount of wiggling, slobbering, etc. Love, I suppose.

We must first distinguish between the telephone and the telephone company. The telephone company is roundly disliked by a great many people. It is a company, after all, and companies in general come in for a lot of dislike. The telephone company like any company is an abstract organizational principle put into effect by individuals, its employees. It is the only phone company in town. It has stockholders and long lines.

The individuals who put the principle into effect are of diverse character but submit to at least one generalization. The individuals who install and service the equipment—those who drive trucks and climb poles—are in general pleasant, agreeable people. The ones who occupy the "business office" generally are not. There are, of course, reasons. But the pleasantness and unpleasantness are greater than that justified by the reasons.

There is a third class of employee, the operator class, which suffers the abuse and ill will generated by the "business office" in the great American public. This is unfortunate, because the operators are often quite congenial. They are congenial in the face of the (easily intuited) threat of losing their jobs should they do something unseemly, like laugh. What with the breakdown of institutions, this type of raucous behavior is becoming more common. I recently had a very pleasant conversation with an operator on the merits of Austin's "gold building" (it appealed to me, but not to her).

For many years I have heard people express their dislike of the company. I have heard artfully rendered accounts of their conflicts with the company. The company always came out on the short end. I cannot gather the energy to defend the company; I do not like it much either. The only thing I can see to suggest about the company is to dissolve it and find some other abstract organizational principle to put in its place.

This new principle would have as its philosophical origin the idea that how long some person talks to another person should in no way be affected by how much money they have. This principle would have as its goal giving away the equipment and the capabilities of the equipment. This principle would maintain the practice of sending out telephone bills because the bills are handsome and it's nice to get mail. There'll be no more of this silliness about paying, however.

I feel certain that if those undeniably brilliant types at Bell Labs could be put on the problem, they could come up with such a principle and put it into operation. Lickety-split.

So much for the company. The telephone itself sits by the desk (on the floor, in the nook, on the hall table), looking for all the world as if it is about to start jumping, wiggling, yapping, and slobbering. It is not, of course. All it will do is ring. The ringing can make you nervous, depending on your proximity and your personality. But this anxiety is minimized by reaching around under to the serrated wheel next to the "loud" arrow and turning it backward. (Recall, if you will, that in cartoons a ringing telephone is shown jumping, wiggling, and shaking.)

Which fails to bring us to the telephone and the concept of the hero.

There are two ways in which the telephone bears relation to the concept of the hero. The first is that the telephone encourages hero formation. The telephone enables a great many people to talk to a great many others very easily. They talk about themselves or other people. Since a hero is created by some people talking about other people, or more precisely, one other person, the creation of a hero is facilitated. However, so many heroes are created that the concept of the hero is devalued in the process.

The other way in which the telephone affects the concept of the hero is that the hero is further devalued because he is accessible. You can call him—or her—up. This explains the unlisted number. This also explains the "hold" button, the answering service or device, as well as a call I made to an illustrious academic five years ago. An English-accented female voice came on the line and informed me that "Mr. X is not the sort of man who likes to talk on the telephone." Heh. Someone in your world actually said that.

Like a million other form-content equations, we are finding this one easily reversible. Should you for some reason wish to be a hero here in the land of heroes, it is ridiculously easy to arrange. Sixty years of movies and thirty years of TV have been helpful in this regard. After you've mastered the brooding silences, the tinge of madness, the refined sensibility, the pointed nonchalance, the aphasia, the drug arrest, the manslaughter charge, and the psychiatric interlude, you'll want to install your telephone equipment. Start with at least four or five lines so you'll get a nice row of buttons across the bottom. A secretary might help, but they're expensive. Beware of the zany message on your answering machine; it's been done to death. Location is an important consideration. Installation in a closet (any enclosure—box, file cabinet, refrigerator) is a nice effect, but the floor (the film *Blowup*) or a hanging basket (another film, *Shamus*) will serve. Don't hesitate to add little touches of your own. You too can play. It's simple.

"Mother, how will I know when I am a great woman here in America?"

"My dear, you will know you are a great woman here in America when you depress the lever, lean into the intercom, and say: 'Miss Bik, hold all my calls.'"

[1975]

Kung Fu Defended

I didn't bring this up. This was brought up in the February 12 issue of *Newsweek* by someone using the pen name "Cyclops" to write television criticism. This Cyclops person up and criticized *Kung Fu*, which was his first mistake. Now if this mistake hadn't caught up, in its way, every single thing wrong with all contemporary writing about television, as well as all American, Malay, high, low, pop, counter, and instant culture and all other kinds of culture everywhere which don't come to mind right away, then I wouldn't bother you with it. But it did. It did, my children.

Kung Fu is a television series starring David Carradine as Kwai Chang Caine, an American-Chinese half-breed who back in the old days in China killed a deserving victim who happened to be the emperor's nephew. This event occurred, near as I can place it, sometime in the late 1860s. Well, things took their inexorable course. Caine lit out for America to do some heavy wandering ("What will you do?" "Wander—rest when I can."), and the emperor offered a Chinese reward and issued rudimentary wanted posters.

Caine is a priest. He is also inscrutable—he was trained in China. But all these Wild West guys just blunder right in trying to scrute him. They all do it. Oh God, think of the ramifications for real life! But the thing about Caine is that everything is right there on the surface, right where you can see it. It's your responsibility to learn how to look. If Caine wanted Oreos, you could see it right there in his eyes, if you knew how to look.

All of this is enhanced by what "Cyclops"—can I call him "Ed"?—by what Ed calls "night-school notions about Buddha, Confucius and Lao-tse" and "the artiest camera work on television today." Caine has stunningly vivid slow-motion flashbacks to China and his friends and teachers there. When he's forced to use his dreaded kung fu powers, a lot of the action is in slow-motion. It's stylized, all right. It's pretentious, all right. Other things which are stylized and pretentious: *Ulysses*, *Hawaii Five-O*, Shakespeare, Pepsi-Cola. Things not stylized or pretentious: trees, venereal disease. And if you want to get deep into Mahayana Buddhism, you're out of luck.

Occasionally Caine tries to look up his distant American relatives. Occasionally he straightens out some of the petty downbeat conflicts of the people he wanders among. Not that he's pushy; he just gets forced into it. And about once per episode Caine does something really spectacular, like taking arrows out of the air with bare hands, or walking through a pit of rattlesnakes. Not a feeble dozen or so; this was a good forty rattlesnakes—western diamondback, if I'm not mistaken, *Crotalus atrox*. Which is to say, "our most dangerous snake" (A. H. Wright and A. A. Wright, *Handbook of Snakes*, 2 vols. Ithaca: Cornell University Press, 1957). Caine has never read Wright and Wright, of course, but he understands. These are heavy snakes. Quickly he flashes back to China where he learned that snakes were just like everybody else, just trying to get by. He knows these snakes. And he respects them. He takes the long walk slowly, carefully, clearly so as not to step on his brothers because, clearly, he does not want to hurt them.

Ed, on the other hand, used to review television for *Life*. Now he has moved to *Newsweek*. *Newsweek* calls him a "provocative . . . critic" of "the most powerful cultural force in the United States today."

Ed's ideas:

First-rate program: *Carol Burnett*

Insulting rhetoric: "[X has] plots dreamed up by empty Coke bottles."

Acceptable reason for watching: "You learn something."

Characteristic wit: "tube-boobie."

To be candid: Ed has never had an interesting idea about television in his life. But that's all right. When he went stomping through the snakes, one *Crotalus atrox* would let him have it. It's even all right that he has this position to abuse; why fight it?

But Ed's simple-minded moral attitude is representative. It is found not only in most other television criticism but also in almost all discussions of television. At a recent meeting of what I took to be the local Austin cultural elite to discuss the possibility of getting a public-access channel out of the local cable company (since arranged, cable channel 10), a boy didn't even want to ask whether all this meant they were going to take off *The Rookies*, so oppressive was the atmosphere of doing good and fixing "the community." Not everyone there shared this attitude (I hope, I guess), but any diverging views were clearly not going to receive a fair hearing. One person who seemed to be asking intelligent questions (which, unfortunately, ran counter to the mood of the moment: does the FCC have any authentic power to enforce its regulations? Is Austin in the top one hundred markets to which a specific regulation applied? Answers: sort of, and no) was met with polite distaste. I am not opposed to public access, which seems a fine idea—and after all there are plenty of channels—but it isn't hard to intuit what public access programming is likely to look and sound like in practice.

Florida is, in fact, the seat of the uptight national sickness of glare-ism. Everywhere you look—GLARE, and much of it unconscious! Well, the solution to this vicious community problem has been worked out in our eclectic Rogerian personal growth groups in which we became less concerned with leaders and individuals and our self-esteem was lowered. We have decided to throw Florida into the Gulf of Mexico, with a big rock tied on to make sure it stays down. Of course we're meeting resistance from the fascists and their dupes, the citizens of Florida, but the people will win out!—we're digging at night.

Or maybe an ongoing 120-part series called *The Sins of Roy Butler* (mayor and Republican). Readings from Herman Hesse accompanied by colored lights! A guitar-playing, all-natural banana! Giving birth standing up!

As is characteristic of moralists and also of theorists of the alternate culture, there are certain basic assumptions which 1) go unexamined, and 2) must be imposed on everyone else. Relating to television, the first assumption is that commercial TV is garbage. Nicholas Johnson is one of the few who can be credited with spending any effort on explaining why (it sells a "philosophy of life" which includes the idea that one's level of consumption of products is the measure of personal worth), most just assume it. If Johnson's book, *Test Pattern for Living*, fits neatly between *Love Story* and *I'm OK, You're OK* on the shelves, it still represents an effort and a gesture of goodwill. The point where goodwill becomes coercive ("we have to educate the people") is where the others start out.

I can't help but notice, additionally, that nothing is required of the viewer past the first simple judgment: commercial TV is garbage. No intelligence, no imagination—the judge might as well be a brick. The process involved is akin to strangling a cat because he doesn't spit silver dollars. Each judge, of course, strangles in his own way ("tube-boobie") and so the strangulation is a tremendous personal expression. No one considers whether strangling was the only way to deal with the cat. No one noticed that while he didn't spit silver dollars, he was an accomplished juggler and grand prix driver and could sing "Nadine" in four languages.

Now the cat strangler/television critic will tell you that he appreciates all this, that he recognizes the evils of "linear" thinking (perhaps somewhat less than its virtues), that he hates and abhors moralism and avoids making "value judgments," that he detests propaganda, that he despises coercion, that he only seeks personhood and freedom for all. Do not believe him. People (I have noticed) will tell you they know things that they do not know, or have not adequately dealt with. A boy goes to these meetings and feels like he is being asked to board the bus which is going to roll across the bay—suggesting that buses don't float is met with derision—"We know that," you are told, just before everyone drowns.

What Ed and these others ask television to provide, then, is a sort of intellectual (moral, political) vitamin on the way to personhood (heaven, utopia, fulfillment). For him, "entertainment" is limited to comedy and comedy to its lowest or basest form—slapstick. He can like Carol Burnett; he accepts his baser nature. For other types of programming he is compelled to find a moral justification. His whole act is being a passive recipient of wisdom, but in the case of television he'll condescend, and take information. Ed explains the failure of Kung Fu and the criteria for success: "We like information, cram courses in other people's social reality, institutional lowdown, the mechanics of a situation. ('So that's how it's done.') It is the basic appeal of the few flourishing popular fiction forms today: detective novels, science-fiction novels, pornography, and Arthur Hailey."

Ed has apparently never heard of dictionaries, almanacs, trade papers, encyclopedias, collections of letters, memoirs, a two-volume series called *The Way Things Work*, documents, in fact, of any type, or looking out the window. Maybe he lives in New York, and doesn't have any windows.

His feeling for information or data is open to question. Give me, for instance, someone who has "night-school notions of Buddha" before someone who tries to tell me that the basic appeal of pornography is that "we like . . . cram courses in other people's social reality." This kind of falsification of data is insidious and implies the moral imperative, the compulsion to make everything fit into a pre-existing theory. Let me suggest that the appeal of detective novels, science fiction, pornography, and Arthur Hailey as well as many good films and most good television is some combination of sex, violence, accessibility, and vicarious emotion. They also have a low-grade order (conventions) which we all recognize. The order is pleasing and reassuring. It is also simple enough that we assume it, and are then free to get to the emotion, sex, and violence, and to appreciate the grace with which the whole project is carried out.

One of the conventions of television is that it is required, as a mass medium, to make extensive gestures in the direction of the triumph of moral man, fair play, evil getting its own reward, sex in love the only good kind and all the other official party-line moral certainties—the accumulated wisdom of F. W. Woolworth. These certainties are attractive; most of us would like to believe for sixty minutes that evil guys eventually get it, even if we reserve the right to define "evil" the way we please. At the same time, commercial TV has become adroit in minimizing these gestures. Most programs just use them as a structural device so that characters screw and consume and kill throughout the show and get nailed at the end. A sop is thrown to official morality so that they can get to what the audience wants to watch. The degree of grace with which these pieties are included adds an extra criterion for judging the production.

Kung Fu in particular takes these values (or variants—principles tend to blur at a distance) and actively uses them. It is an artful synthesis in which morality creates a superman: James Bond. This little irony does a lot to energize the show. And like James Bond, Bogart, John Wayne, or Dennis Weaver's Sam McCloud, Kwai Chang Caine is a heavily stylized hero—one tends to respond because of the stylization. Earlier episodes of the series were less wonderful than later ones because in them this quality was less pronounced. But you know, when Caine approaches an enraged, rearing, no-one-else-can-handle-him horse, that pretty quick that horse'll discover inner peace. And when the six foolish creeps start out to stomp Caine to death, it's only a question of which hand he's going to use—the pleasure is in watching him do it.

There is an essential similarity between McCloud telling some art gallery fop, "I guess that means we're on opposite sides of the barb wahr," and Caine noting, "To the flea, the grasshopper sounds as thunder." If the one is New York's idea of New Mexico and the other is Los Angeles' idea of China and neither is exactly profound, the pretense is still not coercive. Contrast the pretense of Erich Fromm, quoted in Nicholas Johnson's book: "Why is it that we, having everything one could wish, are unhappy, lonely, and anxious?" (from *The Revolution of Hope*).

Is it necessary to point out that Erich, aside from the gigantic diagnosis, is sadly deficient in the wishing department? I mean, I looked all over, the closets, under the sink, and there was no Veruschka anywhere. Intelligent conversation still comes from only the same six people ("Don't call during *Hawaii Five-O*"). The '66 Continental with the Ruidoso Jockey Club sticker on the windshield? Still down at the Gulf Station.

The fact of the matter is that we have created a concept of profundity to protect us from what it intends to describe. Whether the concept is used viciously as in the Fromm quote or frivolously as in the other two gets to be a key question. While Sam McCloud and Caine would allow you to read Erich Fromm, it is doubtful whether Erich Fromm would allow you to watch *McCloud* or *Kung Fu*. And you can think (if you feel like it) as "deeply" and as freely about either as you can about things like, "Why is it that we, having everything one could . . . etc." because thinking is something you do yourself, if you feel like it.

[1973]

The *Newsweek* Short Story: Celestial Puzzler

"I can make a story out of a doorknob.
If it turns, a cover story!"
—*R. L. Bechtold, 1974*

Sales of microscopes trebled, Palomar swinging in its great and graceful arc, strange sights in the night streets of American cities—all these are being attributed to the projected appearance of the first major comet in sixty years. A celestial happening, the Comet Kohoutek, named after Russian astrologer O. (Phil) Kohoutek who first discovered the new light last February, may show up.

In Trenton, astralphilosopher Philip Merrill predicts that the comet will spread "new light" on New Jersey, Cleveland, and the Snake delta, three areas of geopolitical interest where his nonsectarian group has its strongest following. Kohoutek is projected by most scientists to be "at least" six feet long, which might make it the brightest star in the firmament, if it ever appears. It will, if predictions are realized, cover half the sky, which is twelve feet at sundown and eleven and a half feet at sunup, a freaky astrophysical oddity which has puzzled scientists for centuries. This new comet, coming as it does, after Christmas, seems certain to clear that up.

Aristotle Comets have appeared before in history and the lore is rich. Who ever heard of poor lore? In 18 BC a comet appeared over Cincinnati and killed nineteen people, the entire population at that time. The philosopher Aristotle observed that comets often have a long trailing thread behind them, which he christened "the tail." In 44 AD the appearance of the Comet Whistle sparked the hordes of Attila in the sack of Rome. Whistle later reappeared in 415 coinciding with a mysterious tooting and pounding in the heads of humanity. Jurist Garret Augustus Hobart (before he became vice president) is said to have spoken fondly of "comets and shit like that." Comments on comets have been condensed in a slim volume which is used as a bible by inmates of the Colorado Department of Corrections. A recent popular opinion cross section shows seventy-nine percent with "no opinion" pointing to the wide spread of ignorance about comets.

But perhaps the most mysterious phenomenon associated with the celestial pranksters occurred in 1910 with the appearance of Harry's Comet. On March 12, at its apogee (point closest to the sun in an elliptical orbit), Harry blazed so bright in the sky that Franklin, Pennsylvania, up to that time an industrial boomtown of near a million population, disappeared. In the following forty-eight hours, seventy-six members of the Franklin Philharmonic Orchestra, on a road show engagement in Toledo, were snubbed out without so much as a trace. Modern histories make no mention of Franklin, which speaks to the totality of the devastation. Some historians will admit to peculiarity in off-the-record conversations with reporters. In 1898 the Peerless Motor Company was formed.

Physics: There has been much speculation as to the material nature of comets, from the libertine sixteenth century physicist Philp Zent's formulation "anything with a tail" to some modern French metaphysicians who insist that "not is comet is not." In between, more moderate observers take a gentler view. Astronomer Philip Lynch of Los Angeles' Pistello Observatory settles back in his worn Naugahyde chiffonier and expresses a common position: "Comets are tricky. Comets are any color they want." NASA physicists Philip Dempsey and Philip Tegler disagree: "Comets are yellow, infrequently blue. That's it, bucko." Philip Pierce, head of the Pierce Institute in Scottsdale, suggests that comets "are composed of chunks of matter no larger than a tractor," and that these chunks are surrounded by a white-hot syrup of celestial ice which he describes as "about the viscosity of peanut butter, only white." It tastes, Pierce adds, "like fried chicken." Philip Fenner, truculent and diminutive shortstop of the famed British Research League has spent years following comets across their celestial playground. His crack research team is ready with millions of dollars' worth of equipment for Kohoutek, although he hasn't spoken a word since 1942. Amid this honest play of divergent opinion, there is one thing that Dempsey, Tegler, Merrill, Lynch, and most other scientists would agree on—Kohoutek's appearance, should it occur, will be the opportunity of a lifetime.

Real putrid: Perhaps the most provocative theory of all is propounded by an austere, reserved, thin de-metaphysicist from California, the maverick scientist Philip Smith. Smith, a sort of technocrat-*cum*-guru to the caterwauling young, has suggested that other scientists and news reports concerning Kohoutek have ignored the obvious "as usual" and overlooked the most significant aspect of the celestial foie gras. "Comets stink," Smith said from his tree-shaded home on the beach west of Oxnard. "And Koytik is very likely to be real putrid, the worst. Emerson had something to say on this. Koytik's new, and we have no way of gauging comets, today, but it's the newest and largest, and we can't just close our eyes as we have for so long. They do stink and I don't care if you all hate me." The iconoclast's viewpoint is not shared by many; Rotan and Mosle of MIT's Oddlot Labs are among the few colleagues to take Smith's warning seriously. "Phil and I suggest that Smith's in the area of rightness, not perhaps entirely correct, but with some particle of the truth. He may overestimate the extent, but odor will be a significant factor." Rotan and Mosle suggest incense or bacon burning during the apogic period (three to four hours). Smith leans to more drastic measures, followed already by some of his more ardent young disciples, such as rhino-ectomic surgery.

Religious significance: For many, Comet Kohoutek has taken on an extra dimension of meaning. In the Vatican, rumors have been circulating for months about the bald-pated figure dashing along that city's tiny alleys, pounding the bricks with a small hammer. In Baltimore, many persons have been moved to walk the streets on their heads. "The Lord is angry," says sectarian prelate Philip Paine. "He has sent this celestial freak as an emblem of His anger. Many have come to us to learn the secret of head-walking, but most are unwilling to make the sacrifice." Paine, and his general secretary, Philip Webber, have appealed to the Baltimore City Council. The councilmen thus far remain adamant in refusing softer streets.

Celestial poseur: Whether Baltimore's City Council relents or millions of Americans yield to nasal amputation is left to fate and the next few weeks. We will soon know. The onrush of Comet Kohoutek is inexorable and rushing on, and according to reputable authorities it is likely to light the heavens as nothing before or since. The celestial poseur may appear near Orion or, as experts suggest, in the vicinity of the Pleiades—the daughters of Atlas turned to stars in Greek mythology of which six are seeable with average eyes. The wisest words may have been offered by Phyllis Jackson and Phil Curtis, discovered at their chic Central Park West hideaway, who commented, when asked about the greatest celestial pilgrim in our century, "Well, a celestial pilgrim's better than nothing."

Don't Move: A Memoir

Looking back (we discourage looking forward), one is comfortable in the feeling that they've been a good fourteen years, and that they have been this way for one quite simple reason—finding one's niche. Yes, the life of the ne'er-do-well. Failure is a rich and fertile field relatively under-explored except by our novelists who insist on failing in such grand and grandiloquent terms that their failures are useless to the rest of us. I mean, who cares, really, about his identity? Sophomores.

Early on, the ne'er-do-well should be distinguished from the derelict. In romantic moments, I used to fancy myself a derelict, with stubble and eyes streaked in red, tubercular and twitching, filthy dirty and splashed across a four-page full-color spread in *Vogue* with Jean Shrimpton in tow. How the ladies do like violation! But clearly this is not the case, so clearly in fact that I have relinquished the term altogether. A derelict has a lot of integrity and pathos and things of that kind, things I'm sure which are sticky and obvious, things which you can't rid yourself of (if you take a mind to) by flying to Albuquerque. A derelict usually has a bottle of cheap whiskey and an old coat, neither of which I have ever felt much attraction toward except at parties where there are inevitably many bottles of whiskey which the host resents your taking with you. And if you have an old coat, you have to stand around outdoors a lot, and I hate the cold like nothing else.

Derelicts inevitably, too, have some sort of tragic past, something I can't manage, unless you count the nuns on the back (112), but then derelicts tend not to worry about things like nuns, they tend to have real problems. They also have a kind of vulgar authenticity like that of the zealot, but the value of authenticity, clearly, has been blown all out of proportion in recent years. Just as failure is a richer phenomenon than success in the great majority of cases, so the fraud outshines the real. If reality were all that sweet, who would bother with fantasy?

Further, derelicts tend not to have any money, which is a major pain, and which one finds oneself unable to support as a continuous condition. Life without money, as my old friend Anita Bryant is fond of saying, is like a day without sunshine. Who needs it? The only thing worse than not having any money is looking like you don't have any money, because then you're just about cut off from getting any. No one ever accepts a bad check from a wino, but a clean shirt and a driver's license (good for four years) will work wonders. America trusts you.

Now, the life of the ne'er-do-well is more complicated today than it was fifty years ago. Don't you know? The basic new element in the life of the hardcore ne'er-do-well is the proliferation of other ne'er-do-wells crowding up the act. There are actually more bush league derelicts than pure ne'er-do-wells, but it's not a distinction the public makes easily. The bush leaguers themselves often fail to distinguish between the two, actually quite different, fields. A particularly resistant strain of imitation has arisen, conveniently described by the term "committed," which means, basically, that they will kill you for an idea. A kind of personality which has always made me uncomfortable. They do not care about finesse or performance; they care about the ecology. Or sexism. Fine, fine, fine, but it's clouding the public's notion of the ne'er-do-well, and as a consequence, one is invariably confronted with these subjects when all he's trying to do is hustle a meal. Spaghetti is all right so long as while you are eating it you don't have to discuss vaginal politics, a subject, I confess, which has always seemed fairly simple to me. Open and shut. But people nowadays just can't tell the true-hearted ne'er-do-well from his committed, well-pimpled brother. A lot of extra TV sets and broke-down radios and cans of chili go astray, I'll tell you.

The first task for the apprentice ne'er-do-well is to get himself one, two, or six girlfriends who work. This is a delicate problem, because girlfriends tend to lord it over the poor ne'er-do-well and don't much like him splitting up his allegiance. The ne'er-do-well would do well to remember the old saying, "why buy the cow when you can get the milk for free." Don't drink the milk if the cow is unemployed. Almost by definition, a ne'er-do-well is required to be supported by the sweat of a beautiful woman, than which sweat there is perhaps none sweeter. Maybe you saw the Carroll Baker version of *Harlow*; remember the stepfather. Also, while it is true that presently there are a lot more working women, there are fewer and fewer with enough self-hatred and self-doubt. They're all certain they are Mary Magdalene, in the "after" pose. This is surely very healthy for them, but it presents a real problem for you. The show needs to be revised. Paul Newman no longer amuses them—the style is more Dustin Hoffman. You're ugly, but you have "character." You're rotten in bed and you cry over animals a lot. You can get into a rage over oil spills or the trans-Alaska pipeline. You're working on the chemistry of an idea for a way self-esteem might be added to bread. You know exactly what a berserk Swedish bank robber means about Western Civilization. In fact, you spend most of your time reading the *Washington Post* and *HuffPo* in states from euphoria to tears. In other words, manic-depressive in a Che Guevara suit.

The great fear of any ne'er-do-well worth his salt is that he will succeed. A man may spend a lifetime learning the art of failure only to blow his brains out when met with success. And the danger is a very real one in our culture where the happy dilettante may at any moment fall in front of the capricious cameras and have a half dozen microphones pushed at him by a half dozen jerks. The jerks wish him to have opinions because that is their job. The ne'er-do-well knows that he does not need the opinions but he is seduced. Suddenly, he is a success. Whole new attitudes are required. A closet of new quips. He gets a job. Buys a Volvo. Shoots himself.

The true work of the authentic ne'er-do-well is to wander. Wandering is best accomplished if some vague order is given to the activity, in the manner of the classic "quest." The trick is to be on a quest with no object. No white whales, if you please. With no object, you can hardly succeed. Or perhaps it is only that the quest must be for an object without any pretense, a simple or common goal. Money is good in this context. Rain. The wandering which is the central exercise of the ne'er-do-well is not the "wild odyssey, sex drugs truth" version popularized in the fifties and sixties, but more an across-town style. When you find yourself standing somewhere trying to figure a socially acceptable rationale for standing there, you have hit it. Wandering does occasionally bring you face-to-face with conflict. Go around it. All that is required is the answers to a few modest questions, and you have years to work on them. Your fellow man always asks the same questions—it's amazing. What do you do? Do you want to go? Can I help you?

In a humane spirit the ne'er-do-well usually answers his fellow man on approximately the desired level of complexity. I'm a broker, no, no thank you. The ne'er-do-well is always civil; it is his code. But occasionally he must also speak the truth: I stare, I'm sick, and penicillin.

Or, something else.

Biographical Note

Steven Barthelme has published short stories extensively in periodicals, in Pushcart and other anthologies, and in the collection *And He Tells the Little Horse the Whole Story.* A memoir, *Double Down,* co-authored with his brother Frederick, was issued by Houghton Mifflin in 1999. With a long-time interest in non-fiction, he has written pieces for the *New York Times Magazine, Los Angeles Times, Washington Post, Texas Observer, Oxford American,* and other newspapers, magazines, and quarterlies. He writes and teaches in Mississippi.